TIME

UNITING AN AIRLINE AND ITS EMPLOYEES IN THE FRIENDLY SKIES

FOREWORD BY WALTER ISAACSON

OSCAR MUNOZ

FORMER EXECUTIVE CHAIRMAN
AND CEO OF UNITED AIRLINES

WITH BRIAN DESPLINTER

HARPER
BUSINESS

An Imprint of HarperCollins*Publishers*

HarperCollins books may be purchased for educational, business, or sales promotional use. For information, please email the Special Markets Department at SPsales@harpercollins.com.

FIRST EDITION

Designed by Kyle O'Brien

Library of Congress Cataloging-in-Publication Data has been applied for.

ISBN 978-0-06-328428-9

23 24 25 26 27 LBC 5 4 3 2 1

To my United colleagues

Wherever you may be in the world when these words find you, know that you carry with you my gratitude for keeping the New Spirit of United alive, in clear and stormy skies. The generosity you have shown me is a blessing beyond counting. The gratitude I feel to each and every one of you is beyond measure. I hope you know I consider every day before I joined the United family as only a prologue in my life story and every day since an epilogue to the adventure we shared. Together, we set out to change United Airlines. In the end, United changed me, forever and for the better.

CONTENTS

FOREWORD

As a biographer, I am intrigued by the minds of people who've changed the world, especially those who were able to do so because they saw things differently from the rest of us.

Leonardo da Vinci's fascination with the way light plays upon the folds of a curtain informed his study of optics and ultimately revealed to him the secret of projecting three-dimensional images upon a two-dimensional surface.

As a patent examiner, Albert Einstein looked at proposals for devices that used signals to synchronize distant clocks and discovered the theory of relativity, which changed our understanding of time.

Steve Jobs, placing a 1960s garage-band twist on the ancient philosophical conception of the liberal arts and the unities between them, married technological innovation with artistic sensibilities.

From Ada Lovelace in the Romantic Age to Jennifer Doudna in the gene editing age, my biographies tell stories about the life of the mind.

But this book by Oscar Munoz focuses not on the mind but on the heart—and by that word, I refer to both its meanings, the corporeal and the metaphorical.

It's become common to make an analogy between Oscar's near-fatal heart attack and the troubled state of United Airlines when he took over in 2015 and to make comparisons between the company's revival and

Oscar's own courageous recovery from a heart transplant, which occurred in tandem.

Oscar has told me that he believes that the support of his employees helped him pull through; and from my position as a board member of the company, I know that many United employees drew personal inspiration from his health crisis and credit his fortitude with helping the company's revival.

Of course, Oscar survived his heart attack thanks to the genius of doctors, nurses, and caregivers, not merely to well-wishers. And United emerged from its many crises, as well as a pandemic, not simply because of a kinder leadership. It became the strong company it is today thanks to the technical know-how of thousands of aviation professionals, the acumen of financial and business experts, and the caring service of frontline staff.

This book is the compelling personal survival story of Oscar, which anyone who's been touched by cardiac care will find riveting. It is also a comprehensive story of the corporate revival of a great American company, filled with lessons for other leaders.

It offers a fascinating primer into the complexities of the airline industry and the intellectual challenges of running a global operating company, one that flies hundreds of millions of people each year.

But mainly this is a story about heart. Heart is the secret of United's turnaround. It is about the connections that were forged between the thousands of women and men of United Airlines and Oscar, who nearly died before they even got to know him.

From my position on the United board, I have had the opportunity to compare the leadership style of Oscar with those of other prominent chief executives whom I've profiled—in Big Tech and many other fields also.

In writing about such people, a biographer must focus not only on leaders but also on the role of the people they lead. It is the rare memoir written by a CEO that genuinely achieves this. Oscar has done so. He wrote this book the way he captained United. He puts employees at the center of the action, not himself—and rightfully so, for employees are the true heart of the company, and its success belongs to them.

Over the years, I had the good fortune to watch how Oscar forged connections with United's employees, made the sprawling operation feel like a family, and gave it a renewed lease on life. His book explains both how he did it and what lessons we all can learn about leading from the heart.

Walter Isaacson

INTRODUCTION

If you're like most frequent fliers, you probably race through the airport, laser-focused only on what's necessary to reach your gate as quickly as possible. When you're the CEO of an airline, on the other hand, you notice everything. You keep your eyes open for every opportunity to learn something new. You overhear countless conversations—yes, often complaints—that help you improve and serve both your customers and your employees better.

That's the approach I took from day one—to listen, learn, and only then try to lead.

Though time has passed since I bid a fond farewell to my United family in May 2021, even now I can't help but pay attention to the little things when I fly the Friendly Skies, the details that only those who've had the privilege to work in this industry tend to notice.

Not every time, but perhaps the next time you fly, I invite you to unplug the earbuds, slow down your pace, and allow yourself to become aware of what's going on around you as you walk the terminals. You'll suddenly notice the million daily dramas that are unfolding, from the curbside to the concourse and up into the clouds.

You'll witness small, surprising acts of kindness. For example, I'll never forget an occasion when I was chatting with a few gate agents behind the counter and a valued first-class passenger approached to ask to switch seats with a person in military uniform who had been assigned to coach, insisting that we tell no one about the gesture. We obliged on both counts.

Then there are grand acts that have life-changing value. Like the occasion when a family, desperate for time because of a late connection, caught the attention of a customer service representative and explained that if they missed this final flight of the evening, their child wouldn't get to a specialized hospital in time for a crucial treatment. Instantly, United employees formed an ad hoc tactical unit—"Team: Get This Family There"—communicating with the pilots in the cockpit to hold the plane, coordinating with security, commandeering a cart to rush them to the gate, and making sure the staff at the destination airport were aware of the situation and ready to take care of the family when they landed.

A few days later, the parents reached out to thank the employees involved and let everyone know that, because of their effort, their son had received the vital care he needed and was recovering nicely.

While these are *exceptional* stories, they are by no means the *exception*. They are the type of modest miracles that take place every day in our industry.

Whichever airline you fly, I'm sure you hold very strong personal opinions about the airline business. That's because whether it's being present for that wedding or graduation, making it to that once-in-a-lifetime job interview, or getting home in time to tuck the kids in bed, when it comes to connecting you to the people and moments that matter most in life, it's not just business. It's personal. This is the unique role that our employees play in people's lives; it's what elevates the job beyond just a career and into a calling and makes our industry so relevant to so many people.

That is why, in writing this book, my audience is as much a general reader and the flying public as it is the community of airline employees who don't often receive the credit they earn—and who deserve to be reminded, from time to time, of the irreplaceable good work they do every day.

Moreover, insofar as this book focuses on the practice of leadership, the first and most important lesson is that leadership is an act of extended storytelling. Whether it's a president rousing a weary nation to meet a moment of crisis, a coach rallying her tired players to make a comeback in the final seconds of the game, or entrepreneurs risking all they have on a common dream, leaders summon the best out of people by placing present difficulties, however dire, into a narrative that ends, inevitably, in victory and success.

There are many different types of leaders, but the greatest ones I've met have all shared this gift. They have a talent for convincing the people they lead to believe in a shared story and, in doing so, to believe in their own individual abilities to make that story the reality.

That's how United's epic comeback story began. When I became CEO in 2015, I soon realized that I was taking over a United Airlines that, at the time, was anything but united; in fact, it was disunited.

I was no stranger to the airline or its troubles, having served on United's board of directors since it merged with Continental in 2010 and serving on Continental's board for several years before that.

Even as we tried to steer ourselves back on course, our sense of drift increased, veering us far from the golden days when United Airlines was synonymous with "The Friendly Skies," when the very sight of that psychedelic U-shaped tulip emblazoned on all our planes evoked the graceful notes of Gershwin's *Rhapsody in Blue*, filling people with a sense of pride in working for and flying with us.

F. Scott Fitzgerald warned there are no second acts in life. If we were going to convince customers—and the world—that we still had it in us to write a brilliant second act for United, we first had to believe in it ourselves.

It didn't happen overnight, and we experienced many setbacks. But we emerged as a better, stronger airline than we had ever been before because we finally began putting our employees in a place where they felt a genuine pride of ownership over the new United that we were building together.

By early 2020, as I prepared to retire from the company, we had achieved the best relations between management and employees in the industry and reestablished a united front with our three major unions. We had delivered industry-leading stock performance, best-in-the-industry reliability, and ascending levels of customer satisfaction. As the dark clouds of the global pandemic, brought on by COVID-19, began to gather with frightening speed, we knew that the ultimate test of this rebuilt culture had arrived much sooner than anyone expected. I truly believe that if we had not undergone this process of transformation, United might not have survived the crisis.

As I finalize this book at the end of a busy holiday travel season of 2022, I must admit, when I walk through the concourses nowadays, I overhear a more intense frustration from customers directed at all aviation employees, especially as the airline industry struggles to scale up to pre-pandemic capacity.

I empathize with that frustration and, where I can, I try my best to help our employees solve problems, while asking for a little empathy from passengers in return. We are still coming to terms with the extraordinary upheavals that we've experienced, collectively and individually, since the start of the COVID-19 pandemic.

So, as we continue to recover from that turmoil and all it brought with it, I feel this is the perfect moment—an urgent moment—to tell a story that I hope will help heal some of the bonds that have frayed between fellow human beings.

Allow me to tell you about the team of people I had the privilege to lead and how they overcame divisions, worked together, and pulled one of the world's most iconic brands back from the brink of potential failure.

The authorship of the United success story belongs to the tens of thousands of my colleagues who labored to produce it; it is the sum of their actions.

In these pages, I invite you to walk the concourses with me and meet the people who made that turnaround happen, in order to better understand what they do each day to serve you and make the skies a little bit friendlier with each flight, to glimpse what it's like to work shoulder to shoulder and cheek by jowl with people who become your family.

Doctors say that spending a lot of time at altitude changes a person physically. I'm not an expert on that, but I do know—without a doubt—that getting to better understand and appreciate the extraordinary professionals who move metal at 600 miles per hour, and who are most comfortable only when they're at 35,000 feet, has changed me as a human being, forever and for the better.

I hope this book helps more people to respect, admire, and—yes—even love these incredible individuals whose entire vocation is to connect us to the people and places that matter most in life. And, if this story leads all of us to reset our relationships with that cadre of fellow human beings whom we've come to refer to as "essential workers," whatever industry they work in, well, that would be a pretty welcome result, also.

So please allow me to tell you the story of my years spent between the clouds and the concourses and explain how our airline went from looking like it was slouching toward the bitter end of its one-hundred-year journey and somehow found a way to turn itself around, reinvent itself, inspire itself, and emerge as a truly "United" airline.

The FASTEN SEAT BELT sign is now off and you are free to roam about the Friendly Skies in the pages of this book. Bienvenidos, Bienvenue, Willkommen, etc. Welcome.

Oscar Munoz
January 2023

turnaround time: noun: a measurement of the length of time it takes for an aircraft to land, replenish, refuel, and take off for a new flight.

CHAPTER I

ABOVE AND BELOW THE WING

For my money, there's no stage more dramatic, no arena grander or more exciting, than that of an airport. Maybe that's why Hollywood sets so many of its most climactic moments in concourses and gate areas, at ticket counters, and on tarmacs, because that's where the stakes are inevitably highest and every second counts.

Think back on some of the most important, meaningful moments in your life. I'll bet many of them took place within an airport terminal, perhaps one of our last true town squares: joyful reunions and tearful goodbyes, moments of intense frustration followed by elation, long-dreamed-for departures and long-overdue arrivals home, mad dashes to make a flight before the jetway door closes, and those chance encounters with old friends as you rush between gates.

Certainly, many of the most dramatic and pivotal moments that occurred in my life in recent years unfolded either at the airport, on an aircraft, or between the hours of my last touchdown and my next takeoff.

I've experienced moments of literal life and death, surviving a heart attack followed by a heart transplant. I've felt rushes of the highest of career highs as well as the lowest of low points, narrowly defusing potential proxy battles with investors, navigating public relations disasters, and confronting a global pandemic.

Through it all, I had the privilege of serving with the people of United Airlines as they conducted one of the most dramatic and discussed corporate turnarounds in aviation history. As with any big drama, when it comes to running an airline, what transpires backstage is even more fascinating than what the public sees.

Even if you don't follow the airline industry closely and are not a confirmed "av-geek," if you're among the nearly two-thirds of passengers who fly only a few times a year, don't have a MileagePlus account, and haven't a clue how airlines work, still, by picking up this book, I assume you'll have a vague recall of United's resurgent history.

In taking you behind the scenes of that story, I also hope to peel back the curtain on what it takes to run an airline, in smooth skies and choppy ones.

If you happen to be a well-seasoned frequent flier, on the other hand, I hope this book will dispel a few myths along the way and challenge some of the assumptions you may have about our business in a way that surprises and entertains.

And, if you count yourself among the true "road warriors" who fly at least a few times a month, this book will prove that no matter how well you think you understand this industry, there's always something more to discover.

You may well consider yourself such a pro that you could likely make it from the skycap to your usual gate area blindfolded. You've perfected your routine; you've timed out exactly when you need to arrive at the airport; how long it takes to pass through the TSA security checkpoint; where to find the best spots to charge your laptop; you may even know the name of your favorite bartender or barista. You may think you know every inch of your most frequented airports, but I'll bet you've passed by a nondescript door a thousand times in your travels, never giving it a second glance.

Open that door and you are thrust into the midst of a bustling, high-octane world comprising vast labyrinths of maintenance depots and break rooms, control facilities and data centers, warrens of access tunnels and service areas. These are the gears behind the clock face, so to speak, which never stop moving, and they click together to keep our intricate, multifaceted, vastly interesting, nonstop industry performing with the precision of a fine timepiece.

It is an industry that is ever in motion but always positioned firmly at the nexus of the events that shape our lives. The airline business serves as the ultimate leading and lagging indicator of global trends, from geopolitics and economics to the most urgent pocketbook issues. It is a weather vane that shows the direction of travel for our society and a compass that points to what's coming next.

If you're of a certain age, you may remember a famous commercial for United.

Open with: A composer strides across the stage of an elegant symphony hall. Taps his baton on a music stand.

Cut to: The captain on the flight deck pulls an aircraft from the jetway. Suddenly, a passenger, sitting in coach, begins playing those iconic opening notes of Gershwin's *Rhapsody in Blue* on a clarinet. Flight attendants perform last checks, as more passengers join in with their own instruments, first a whole woodwind section, then strings, followed by brass. Outside, on the tarmac, the ground crew guides the plane, waving those orange batons, as the full orchestra swells to a crescendo and the aircraft finally takes off into the sunset.

A clever bit of marketing but a fitting metaphor. It takes hundreds of people, working in harmony, across time zones, to safely perform the roughly half dozen "turnarounds" that a single short-haul aircraft will potentially make each day.

As you walk the concourse, you would never know that you are at the center of that epic performance, and dramas are unfolding just below your feet—what we call "below the wing."

Maintenance crews and technicians, cleaning service personnel and food deliverers, baggage teams and aircraft marshalers, security officers and tug drivers are all working to stay with the meter.

Meanwhile, "above the wing," flight crews are getting themselves into position, and gate agents are making last-minute seating assignments and upgrades.

Like some of the greatest orchestral conductors who often conduct slightly ahead of the beat, the team located at the Network Operations Center (NOC), the cortex from which all United global operations are managed, is constantly at work to remain ahead of the clock.

During my tenure it was housed on the twenty-seventh floor of our headquarters in Chicago's Willis Tower, more commonly known as the Sears Tower.

Resembling a cross between NASA Mission Control and the bridge of the starship *Enterprise*, hundreds of workstations encircled a massive central screen, tracking the real-time positions of every civilian aircraft and weather pattern everywhere on planet Earth.

From the orientation of aircraft to the location of flight crews, from the largest engine parts right down to an individual screw, every asset is constantly tracked and sourced. Operating twenty-four hours a day, 365 days per year, with zero latency, the NOC functions on its own independent power supply and support systems in case of emergency. The redundancies don't end there.

For example, in the small hours of May 18, 2020, massive flooding triggered rolling electrical blackouts across Chicago. In short order, personnel relocated and they were back up and running at our secondary NOC, which was identical to the Willis's in every detail, from the position of every switch and circuit, right down to the location of the coffeemakers and the bathrooms. The sun never sets on the global United network; the concept of "9 to 5" isn't in our vocabulary.

Every minute, everywhere in the airline's network, operational stats tick on monitors wherever our United employees are working, including the all-important D-Zero (D:00) metric. It calculates how closely to the scheduled departure time a flight actually takes off, with a perfect on-time departure designated as 00:00 minutes. Airline people synchronize their entire lives to this ever-changing number, never going more than a few minutes without glancing at the digital counters that act like an EKG for the health of our business.

Any given minute, dozens of flights are taking off and landing around the world, with millions of individual interactions taking place between employees and customers, on the ground and in the sky. That means anything can happen in this business, no two days are ever the same, and we live to expect the unexpected.

As you settle into your seat during the minutes before the aircraft pushes back from the gate, you may find yourself absent-mindedly scrolling through emails on your iPad, making a last-minute call to your spouse or partner, or maybe even leafing through the pages of this book, never realizing you are at the center of this vast, ever-expanding concert.

And as the wheels lightly lift from the runway, a whole new team is preparing for your arrival thousands of miles away, so they are ready to turn your aircraft around again and get it back in the air as safely and efficiently as possible.

This "turnaround time" is the metronome that tracks the pace of life in the industry and keeps our hearts beating to a common rhythm. There are many other measures of success, of course, and by 2018 United was soaring on all of them, regularly setting new operational records, including best on-time departures, most reliable baggage handling, and fewest cancellations in the company's history.

The first glimmers of improvement appeared when our turnaround time started moving in the right direction—it was like the moment when a doctor detects a faint pulse in a patient: we still had life left in us.

Turning around an aircraft and turning around an airline are very different challenges in most respects, save one: it takes a united team to perform it well.

Our planes don't perform turnarounds automatically, and neither did our airline. Instead, it took several years of collective hard work and individual sacrifices.

In the end, we found a way to turn ourselves around as a company in an astonishingly short period, thanks to the determination of our people who worked tirelessly—below the wing, above the wing, and everywhere in between.

CHAPTER 2

"THE HEART HAS RECEIVED MAJOR INSULTS"

Do you know an Oscar Munoz?" It's lucky that my wife, Cathy, answered the landline at all when it rang so early on that Thursday morning.

She was on her way out of the house, about to take a walk around the neighborhood with a pair of her friends, and didn't recognize the caller ID.

The voice on the other end belonged to a nurse from Northwestern Memorial Hospital in downtown Chicago.

She told Cathy that I had sustained a serious heart attack and had been admitted into the cardiothoracic intensive care unit earlier that morning; she should try to get there as soon as possible.

Cathy was with our youngest son, Jack, at our home in Ponte Vedra, Florida, near Jacksonville, where he was a freshman in high school.

Cathy hung up the phone in disbelief. The nurse had told her precious few details about what had happened to me—neither the diagnosis nor the prognosis. She tried my cell phone incessantly, to no avail; obviously something was very wrong.

Could they have the wrong Oscar Munoz? After all, I was healthy and ate vegan, an avid biker and former marathoner; and I had recently completed a hundred-mile bike race. I didn't smoke or drink caffeine, and none of my family members had a history of heart troubles, as far as I knew.

My mother, Francisca, had tragically passed years earlier, when I was twenty-four, but of metastatic breast cancer, not cardiac-related disease. She was only fifty-four, nearly the same age I was on the day of my heart attack.

I never knew my biological father; he and my mother went their separate ways before she gave birth to me in Juárez, Mexico. Facts were sparse and we didn't talk about him at all growing up, though I'd heard that he had also passed away, fairly young—from what I don't know.

In contrast to my own family history, Cathy's was far more conventional—white, suburban, and firmly middle class—as one might notice from our wedding pictures. In August 1984, our two families gathered at the same church in Pasadena where Cathy's parents married each other many years before. Though we'd only met a few years earlier in college, our friends and families had quickly fused into a community, as diverse as we are, with our marriage at the center. So much so, that even though we were married in an Episcopalian ceremony, my traditionally minded Mexican grandmother joked that it could've passed for Catholic, enough to assure her I'd not strayed far from her religion.

For more than thirty years, that extended family kept growing as Cathy and I had children of our own, and we continued to look with optimism toward the future.

Until the phone call that morning, that is. After a moment, Cathy gathered herself and shifted into action mode. She hurriedly packed some bags, picked Jack up from school, and drove to the airport.

Along the way, she called my executive assistant at United, Sonja Ilic, who at that moment was wondering where in the hell I was.

I had failed to show up for an important breakfast meeting where I was supposed to interview a potential hire for the role of chief financial officer—not something I would've blown off.

Over the phone, Cathy—trying to hide the fear in her voice—was wary not to be the source of rumors, even with Sonja, until she had more solid information. Trying her best to answer honestly, Cathy explained that I had injured myself working out and she would be flying to Chicago to take care of me.

Our three older kids each, in turn, received breathless calls from their mother, telling them to meet her in Chicago.

Our oldest, Jessica, fresh from her honeymoon, flew in from Atlanta. Kellie, our next oldest, came from Raleigh, where she had started graduate school at Duke. Kevin, several years younger than his sisters, flew in from Nashville, where he was a sophomore at Vanderbilt.

A few hours later, Jessica touched down at the airport and met up with Cathy and Jack at the arrivals gate—hugs and tears abounding, but also many questions and much panicked theorizing. They shared a tense car ride straight from the airport to the hospital, followed shortly thereafter by Kellie and Kevin.

Once they'd all arrived at Northwestern Hospital, the cardiac interventionist, Dr. James Flaherty, filled them in on the grim details.

That morning, Flaherty explained, a few minutes before eight o'clock, he was alerted that a patient had just arrived at the emergency room and presented symptoms of acute myocardial infarction. He rushed downstairs and burst into the trauma room to find me, lying on a gurney, ashen faced and barely conscious, still wearing my sweaty workout clothes from my morning run.

Disoriented, I had apparently kept muttering something to the effect of, "I don't have time for this, I'm supposed to be at a meeting right now." The nurses had wisely ignored my faint ramblings, and Flaherty ordered me to be moved to the cath lab—the cardiac catheterization laboratory—to perform an immediate angiogram.

My extremely low blood pressure indicated cardiogenic shock, which meant blood and oxygen weren't reaching my brain or extremities. The angiogram revealed a coronary thrombosis—a massive blood clot had lodged itself in my left main artery, blocking more than 70 percent of blood flow.

At some point, my heart stopped completely, and doctors defibrillated me twice to shock it into working again. After intubating me and placing me on a ventilator, Flaherty's team performed an angioplasty by inserting a catheter directly into my heart, which then inflated a tiny balloon that widened the blocked artery. They then placed a stent to keep it open. With that completed, Flaherty next prepped me for a TAVR—transcatheter aortic valve replacement—inserting an artificial valve into my heart.

"The heart has received major insults," he told my family—an unforgettable phrase, apparently a medical term of art, but something that strikes the layperson's ear as both strange and oddly apt.

Cathy and the kids tried to prepare themselves emotionally, but there was no preparing for what they would see when they were finally admitted into my room in the ICU. The sight of me shocked them. Looking back at the pictures from those days, I looked like death.

I lay unconscious, in a medically induced coma, surrounded by a forest of scary-looking medical machines and equipment.

Tubes, IVs, and wires were sprouting from my mouth, chest, neck, and lower extremities. My pulse was so weak that doctors had inserted catheters into my legs because they couldn't find a vein in my arms. My pallor was ghostly white, and my face looked shrunken and hollow.

My lungs were too weak to work, and the ventilator breathed for them. My heart was not working at all, so a tube was inserted into my arteries and connected to an ECMO, an artificial heart and lung machine. Blood flowed through the tube and the machine cleaned and oxygenated it before pumping it back into my system.

The "thrombi," an inch-or-so-long piece of coagulated matter that had been accumulating in my left ventricle, triggered what the American Heart Association refers to as the "chain of survival"—the sequence of events that must occur for a patient to survive. Only one in ten people who experience such a heart attack lives, and unless treatment is administered within the first few minutes of a cardiac episode, the odds of survival drop close to zero.

While a quick response by emergency personnel, rapid transport to the hospital, and access to advanced trauma and life support care are essential to beating these steep odds, the most important link in the "chain of survival" is the very first one: awareness.

Yet, like more than half of all heart attack patients, the sudden cardiac arrest that nearly ended my life that morning arrived with no advance warning or prior symptoms. And, as with the more than 70 percent of people who are mistakenly assessed as "low risk" by traditional measures, my blood work gave me no reason to pursue further checkups that might have detected the clot earlier. Thankfully, new precision medical technologies, powered by artificial intelligence, are changing the way that doctors measure the plaque buildup in the heart's arteries, which would've detected my risk earlier. Medical start-ups are scaling these technologies so more people can understand their own risk profile and preempting any further links in the chain of survival.

If by writing this book I can help even one person take better charge of their heart health care, then it will have been well worth it.

As dire as my situation appeared, thanks to the teamwork of EMTs, nurses, doctors, and staff, I still had a fighting chance, but just.

"He's lucky," Dr. Flaherty told my family. "Moments later may have proven too late."

But I was far from out of the woods. The seventy-two hours after sudden cardiac arrest are the most uncertain, when it is not possible to determine whether the brain sustained serious damage from lack of oxygen and blood flow. Moreover, it would soon become clear that the so-called insults to the heart muscle were so extensive that I would need a transplant if I was going to pull through.

The medical staff prepared my family for the real, perhaps likely, possibility that this story wouldn't have a happy ending.

CHAPTER 3

COMMON METAL

A near death experience tends to make one fatalistic, understandably. I don't go in much for that sort of thing, but even I'll admit that some of the coincidences surrounding my heart attack and heart transplant are a bit spooky.

Every thirty-seven seconds, someone in the United States dies of sudden cardiac arrest, according to my colleagues at the American Heart Association, where I'm now actively involved. As it happens, thirty-seven minutes elapsed between my 911 call and when they connected me to the ECMO, a fact I've confirmed with Dr. Flaherty. And that fateful morning marked my thirty-seventh day on the job as CEO of United Airlines.

Those first weeks at United were a frenzy of nonstop activity, from the moment I walked into the office on my first day to the moment my heart stopped thirty-seven days later.

My first instinct upon taking the job was to get out of the confines of our global headquarters in Chicago as soon as possible. In the two weeks before the heart attack, I had zipped across multiple time zones and points of latitude, visiting with employees and customers at each of our seven domestic hubs spread across the United States—my first chance to introduce myself to the company.

To avoid the look of being walled off by an entourage, I didn't travel with a staff. I didn't want anyone to think they couldn't approach me as I walked by.

I should make it clear that, no, I didn't fly on a corporate jet but rather on our normal service. I took advantage of that opportunity every time I traveled.

Rather than dozing off or catching up on reading, the instant the captain switched off the FASTEN SEAT BELT sign, I took that as my cue to hop out of my seat and make myself available to anyone who might want to chat. I always got a good chuckle when a customer would wander to the galley and discover, to their utter surprise, the CEO chatting with a group of flight attendants, catching up on life and family, talking about everything, and also, about . . . well, not much of anything at all.

There are many perks that come with the job of being chief of an airline, but, for me, the fortuitous exchanges with colleagues—in galleys and on ramps, in break rooms and in jump seats across the system—provided the greatest joys. They also helped me keep up with the pulse of the sprawling global operation.

Of course, I couldn't have navigated my way through the vast United network without Sonja back at the office, pulling the strings, troubleshooting, and stage-managing this global road show I was attempting. She quickly gave up trying to keep me on a tight schedule during airport visits, resigning herself to the fact that, invariably, I'd call a last-minute audible to chat with customers or learn more from an employee. Sonja would have rebooking options ready, without fail.

If an employee raised an interesting issue at a company town hall event or in a private conversation, I'd hurriedly text her with the details of what happened so she could remind me to follow up on the matter.

Many of the issues employees raised were familiar to me already from my experience as a member of the board of directors and chairman of the audit committee.

But you scarcely needed to be a company insider to know that the airline faced serious headwinds or that we had failed to meet the high expectations we had set when United merged with Continental. Employees knew it. Investors on Wall Street knew it. Customers knew it, certainly.

When I transitioned from my position on the board to become CEO in September 2015—taking over from a predecessor who'd departed under the cloud of a federal investigation—I was greeted by an open letter from a prominent Global Service Million Miles customer. Let's just say that it got a lot of press.

"An Open Letter to the New United Airlines CEO or Why I Left United After 3 Million Miles."

Here's how it began:

"Dear Oscar, Congratulations and *condolences* on your new role."

The note didn't get kinder from there.

I asked my team to track down the customer so I could call him, personally. We managed to win him back to United. That was one customer taken care of. I had about 160 million more to go.

Bloomberg Businessweek summarized the state of the airline in a scathing profile. "United's Quest to Be Less Awful," screamed the headline, above a cartoon depicting one of our jets twisted into a knot.

The negative opinions were hard to bear and the facts impossible to argue with.

We consistently trailed our two largest competitors, Delta Airlines and American Airlines, on financial results and stock performance, on-time reliability, and customer service.

United held the ignominious distinction of having the most DOT customer complaints filed against US airlines in 2012 and 2013, and JD Power ranked us dead last among the legacy carriers.

Lucrative corporate customers were threatening to take their business across the street unless they saw dramatic improvements.

The investment community had lost confidence in United's ability to manage itself, to accurately guide for and meet projected earnings, and to deliver on our strategic goals.

Simultaneous negotiations with the leaders of more than a half dozen employee unions had creaked to an acrimonious stalemate after years of turmoil, with accusations of bad faith exchanged by all sides.

For a company called United, ironically, we were riven by deep divisions— between management and employees and between employees and customers. Moreover, employees were bitterly divided among themselves.

Ever since the 2010 mega-merger that was meant to integrate Continental with United, the world watched us struggle, and fail, to unite two large, proud, and often warring groups of employees into a cohesive operational culture.

A sense of rivalry and resentment ran rife on both sides. It was legacy Continental employees, sub-Cons (or "ex-Cons," as they jokingly liked to refer to themselves), versus legacy United employees, or sub-UA. Both are proud communities with rich traditions that are not given up easily. Every friction point between the two work groups imposed steep costs on our operational and financial performance, as well as to our customer-facing service.

Employees had been promised that this would be a marriage of equals. But, as with marriages that get off to a rocky start, both parties mutually felt they had given up more than the other, and each believed they were bending over backward when the other wasn't.

United employees, from their perspective, felt they had to make overnight adjustments to new ways of doing things, namely the Continental way, and they weren't happy about it.

Equally, sub-Con folks bridled at having to adopt and adjust to rules that were carried over from United's previous operation, including the computer systems that dictated how employees could bid to work on the best routes, request schedules and assignments, and even get their paychecks every month. Sub-UA employees felt the same way about the procedures that were ported over from Continental's operation. The truth is, both groups were right, each from their own point of view.

From the perspective of the customer, this dysfunction at the heart of the company was felt in many frustrating ways. For example, if you flew with us during this period, then you probably experienced a time when the gate agent announced that your flight would be delayed because there weren't enough flight attendants or pilots available. Then, you might've looked across the gate area and saw an entire flight crew just waiting around.

"What the hell?" you might think to yourself, rightly. There is an explanation, though not an excuse, for inconveniences like these, which happened with regularity in the post-merger days and seemed baffling in the eyes of customers.

Due to ongoing labor negotiations and unfinalized work contracts, sub-Con employees were not yet allowed to serve on the same aircraft as their sub-UA counterparts, and vice versa. We were not yet flying on "common metal"—metal, in airline parlance, referring to aircraft.

By the time I became CEO, more than five years had passed since the two airlines merged, five years that for our employees and customers felt like one long winter of discontent. The process had stalled, and we were, in effect, two companies that had merged on paper but not in practice. Two airlines, operating side by side, but not flying together.

Management and the front line also didn't seem to be flying together, not sharing common metal ourselves—metaphorically speaking. It was as if we were two separate groups, traveling in opposite directions.

I could feel this culture of separation as I walked the concourses or hung out with employees in break rooms at each of the destinations I visited.

While my arrivals were met with an outpouring of enthusiasm from most employees, filled with high fives, hugs, and selfies, behind the friendly smiles and careful responses I detected a deep well of emotion, pent up by years of feeling unseen, unsung, and unsupported by decision makers at the very top.

Call it intuition—a sixth sense, perhaps. From an anguished look here, a tearful exchange there—a hand that clasped mine a little tighter or held it for a moment longer than usual—I understood that my employees wanted to tell me something I needed to hear, but they held back, slightly—for some reason. That would soon change.

While flying back from Denver to Chicago one afternoon, early in my tour, I strolled through the aisle, chatting with customers and members of the inflight team along the way, as I always do, working my way toward the galley. There I met Amy, one of our Denver-based flight attendants, a veteran of the company.

Our conversation on that flight would mark a kind of "origin story," the genesis of United's turnaround.

I don't have a pre-rehearsed script when chatting with employees. My most insightful prompt is, simply, "Hi, I'm Oscar. How are you doing?"

That was about all it took.

As I asked my question, I could see that she had so much to say to me but wasn't sure if she could—*or should*. She must have seen something as we locked eyes, an invitation assuring her that, indeed, she was among friends and—suddenly—she burst into tears. "Oscar," she said, "I'm just tired of always having to say, 'I'm sorry.'"

In an instant, the barrier between CEO and employee evaporated. I was new to the airline. Yet, as if by alchemy, I felt like I was an old colleague, someone who Amy believed would understand what it is like to invest both heart and soul in a company and not feel any sense of recognition or respect in return.

I am sure if you had been in the galley with me that afternoon, your heart would've broken for her, as mine did. And that's not something I say lightly anymore. She didn't elaborate much further or allow herself to complain. After a few minutes, I promised I would remember her words. We hugged, and with that, she got right back to work serving customers.

I stood in the galley, alone, absorbing what I'd just heard. Over the last couple of weeks, I had gathered information, spoken with hundreds of employees, customers, investors, analysts, consultants, elected officials, union leaders, public relations firms, and all our various stakeholders. I had reams of data, human resource reports, financial analysis, and commentary telling me what was wrong with United.

Yet it took a single frontline employee to crystallize all of it for me, speaking barely above a whisper in the galley but carrying the force of a shout.

It was a watershed moment, and I knew this was a message that would "travel," so to speak. Whatever the language, dialect, or culture, if United employees working anywhere in the world heard what Amy expressed to me that day, they'd wholeheartedly agree with her. And so would customers, I believed.

Ask yourself how many times you have been told some version of the following by an airline employee:

"I'm sorry the flight is delayed." "I'm sorry the coffee sucks." "I'm sorry, I'm sorry, I'm sorry."

"No, we cannot accommodate that request." "No, we can't seat you next to your young child." "No, no, no, no."

Trust me, it is as exhausting for the employee as for the customer; even more so when the employee is apologizing on behalf of decisions being made way at the top, over which they have zero control.

If your flight is delayed or your bags are lost, if the airplane is cramped and crowded or if the amenities have been cut to the bone, frontline employees—especially those who are customer facing—are the ones who receive the complaints. They didn't create the problems, but they're responsible for solving them—and they're told to do it with a smile.

"Be the Brand"—that was the slogan used in our employee communications in those days. It rightfully became a target of mockery. Not because it was a bad slogan, per se, but it implied that all the responsibility of serving customers rested solely on the shoulders of our frontline employees, not shared by management. As if our employees' attitudes were all that stood in the way of winning customers back to United. Not the cost-cutting, rule-obsessed, disciplinary-heavy culture that had come to ill define what it meant to "Fly the Friendly Skies" during those difficult years.

Every time employees learned that another perk had been rescinded or another onerous rule had been imposed upon them or their customers, they would see those posters and shake their heads: "Hey management, practice what you preach."

They weren't looking for an excuse not to do their jobs. They were looking for me and the top brass to do ours—that is, to create an environment where hearing "thank you" becomes the expectation for frontline employees, not the rare exception.

The sense of frustration—betrayal, even—that I heard in Amy's voice reminded me of another conversation I had, with a ramp employee at Chicago O'Hare Airport (ORD) a few days earlier.

Ramp employees are the workers you see when you look outside your airplane window as they work furiously below the wings, loading luggage, deicing the plane in bad weather, and other labor-intensive duties.

This gentleman had decades of service to the company under his belt—sweat equity, in the most literal term. He told me he used to proudly wear his United swag to social events like his kids' soccer games and family barbecues. "Now," he said, "I'd rather people think I'm unemployed than admit I work at United," meaning he simply couldn't bear to listen to another tirade against the service from his family, friends, and neighbors.

When I heard that story, I was pissed off—not at him but on his behalf. I wanted to light a fire under the ass of the person in charge.

Well, now that person was me.

As we descended into Chicago, after speaking with Amy, I was indeed fired up. I felt that I was beginning to distill the volatile mixture of feedback into a digestible solution, one that I could easily communicate to every United employee.

From now on, every decision would have to pass a simple litmus test: Will this put our employees in a better or a more difficult position to serve our customers?

This was the north star I was looking for, and it took one of my employees to point it out to me.

A few days later, I resumed the next leg of my tour, ready to road test this new insight at our hubs—first at Newark Liberty (EWR), then Houston (IAH), Los Angeles (LAX), and San Francisco (SFO).

Each time I stood up in front of a group of employees and got a frosty reception, Amy's words never failed to break the ice. I would see the heads begin to nod and the tone beginning to change.

After two more weeks of traveling, I knew that my time was running out. The board of directors, investors, and my executive team at headquarters were becoming anxious to hear my newfound—though still inchoate—turnaround strategy.

CHAPTER 4

A DAY IN THE LIFE

The day before my heart attack was the prototypical "day in the life" of an airline CEO.

I wrapped up another employee visit at our hub in San Francisco, took off, and landed at O'Hare in the early afternoon.

The chief of our technical operations department met me planeside. I jumped in his truck and the two of us drove across the airfields to the United hangar, where the Tech Ops teams do their highly skilled work—performing maintenance on aircraft, airframes, and engines, as well as on the complex avionics and mechanical systems.

I hadn't had a chance to meet this group of employees yet, and I didn't want to finish my listening tour until I had. A quick food break, with sandwiches and soda, was served, and I had a chance to test run some of my ideas with this team.

Next, I headed to Chicago's City Hall, where I was met by Margaret Houlihan Smith, then managing director of government affairs, and a consummate Chicago political insider. We rode the elevator to the fifth floor to meet with the mayor, Rahm Emanuel.

Chicago is to politics as Paris is to art, as an old saying goes. That was certainly true for Rahm. For decades he had self-consciously cultivated a style that blended the more artful, even performative, aspects of politics with the gritty, hard-edged realism that had made him an effective aide to President Clinton, chief of staff to President Obama, and congressional leader.

We didn't always agree, but I shared Rahm's vision to revive Chicago, its economy as well as public services, in part by attracting high-value corporate relocations that would boost the tax base.

As with every city we serve, especially our hubs, for Chicago to remain the world-class city we both wanted it to be, United would have to play its role, too, and that meant becoming a best-in-class airline once more.

This was a message that I knew would land with my audience at our next stop, just a few blocks away from City Hall, at a meeting of the Executives' Club of Chicago. We entered a ballroom that was packed with the city's most prominent business leaders, a "target rich" audience for the new CEO of the city's hometown airline to meet. I mingled my way through the crowd of bigwigs and found Dave Hilfman, our global head of sales. There's a reason Dave is always chosen to emcee United's biggest events. A showman to his core, whatever fuel source powers Dave's megawatt personality, I'm sure it has a half-life of about ten thousand years. We found him at the center of a large group, of course, regaling his listeners with his sales pitch, peppered with jokes and storytelling flair.

I pulled Dave and Margaret aside for a moment and asked them to point out the top CEOs and business leaders whom I needed to focus on, to convert them from American Airlines customers—our biggest rival at Chicago O'Hare—into United loyalists.

We took the opportunity to invite a few key guests to an impromptu dinner at the nearby Chicago Cut Steakhouse, a venerable establishment overlooking the river and a favorite haunt of the city's politicos.

A few United people were invited, as well as creative and account executives from Edelman, the PR consultancy firm I'd recently brought on board.

I don't remember sitting down but rather playing the role of roving host, walking around the table to talk individually with each person, workshopping the employee-first turnaround philosophy that was taking shape in my head.

Edelman had recently helped me launch "United Airtime," a digital platform for both passengers and employees to "air" their criticisms. The ire from customers was heated but expected: "I felt like an inconvenience, not a customer" was one message that summarized thousands of others like it.

If we were going to win back those customers, I told the group of both Edelman and United folks, we first needed to win back our employees. I told them what I had seen out in the field: the evident pride that I saw in employees when they spoke about their jobs, the cynicism I encountered from both customers and employees when I promised them things would change. I told them about Amy and the new direction in which I wanted to take the company.

I became so engrossed in the discussion that time almost got away from me. I glanced at my phone and saw I had a few hundred emails (literally) to sort through, many of them from customers. I'd want to respond to as many as I could before the end of the night, and I'd have to wake up extra early if I wanted to go for a run before beginning another day with a stacked schedule.

I thanked the service staff for hosting us, as well as Dave and Margaret, and walked out of the restaurant into the brisk fall air, taking a leisurely walk back to my temporary corporate apartment a few blocks away.

• • •

The next morning, October 15, 2015, my alarm woke me at 5:30 a.m., tired and jet-lagged, but brimming with optimism. I immediately picked up my phone and checked the data that was streaming via an encrypted linkup from United's Network Operations Center, the NOC. The real-time dashboard was already flashing red with delays. *Damn, this is going to be a rough day*, I thought to myself.

I laced up my Nikes for my early-morning five-mile run. In the bluish light of dawn, I stepped out of my high-rise building in Chicago's River North neighborhood, jogged through side streets, and merged onto the path that curves along the shores of Lake Michigan, taking in the breath-taking views of the Second City's iconic skyline.

With the greenery of Grant Park gliding by on my right, the waters of Lake Michigan lapping the concrete barrier to my left, I pushed harder, my heart pumping faster and faster. I checked my heart rate monitor and found I was on pace to beat my best time. I preferred to look at my personal "on-time performance" rather than United's that morning.

It promised to be a big day in the history of the company. We had invited all the leaders of our major unions to Chicago, and this would be my oppor-tunity to do what had never been done before—though it was long overdue: to get every union leader into the same room and find common ground, even if it meant being on the receiving end of some pretty heated rhetoric.

As I ran, I glanced over my shoulder at the Willis Tower, formerly the Sears Tower, where United's headquarters were the anchor tenant. Soon, my leadership team would be arriving at the office, and they'd be looking forward to debriefing with me about my travels as well as to prepare for the meeting with union leaders.

They would also want to know how my interview with a potential CFO went that morning—my first appointment of the day—which held special significance beyond the urgent need to fill the role. Within my first days on the job, I received a call from Brad Gerstner, the founder and CEO of Altimeter Capital and a prominent investor in the airline sector.

Despite his stake in the company, a few members of my financial team told me not to bother returning the call; his complaints had become famil-iar to them by now and they'd deal with it for me. I had the good instinct to call Brad right back. I wasn't about to ignore advice from someone with such deep knowledge of the industry and a long track record of success. I'd lived through searing experiences in my career that taught me just how fast and furious an investor's concern can escalate, even sparking a full-blown proxy battle—the absolute last thing United needed.

When I got Brad on the phone, he kindly congratulated me on the new role but told me, bluntly, that he was intent to have his viewpoints heard, not sidelined—as he felt they had been under previous leadership.

I completely understood Brad's position and found it interesting that even a prominent industry investor like him felt that he had been unheard. He was in good company in that regard.

Proof, not promise, is a maxim I try to live by, and I wanted to prove that I was listening and taking his concerns to heart, so I asked him to suggest some people for key positions and agreed to interview someone he liked for CFO. We set up the meeting between myself and Brad's suggested candidate, scheduling it to be the first thing on my agenda when I returned from traveling.

Though it had nothing to do with missing the meeting that morning, in the course of time Brad's firm, Altimeter, would form an investor group with another investment fund, PAR Capital Management, in attempting to change the makeup of our board. But that would be later.

For now, I was still focused on what I'd learned during my visits across the system, and most of all about what Amy had said to me on that flight from Denver.

As I picked up my runner's pace that morning, the sun rising above the horizon of Lake Michigan, I began to imagine what came next: how we might operationalize this still nascent employee-first strategy.

Nearing the end of my run, drenched in sweat, I turned the corner onto Solidarity Drive, the thin half-mile land bridge that connects Grant Park to Northerly Island. On the home stretch, I broke into a full sprint toward the Adler Planetarium, which is perched on an outcrop that overhangs Lake Michigan. As I bounded up the marble steps, my heart was full. Little did I know that, quite soon, it would be my heart that needed saving as much as our airline.

Back in my apartment, about twenty minutes later, I was standing in the kitchen, cooling down, making a smoothie (vegan, of course). I heard my phone ring and assumed it was Cathy calling—we hadn't checked in with each other yet that morning. As I reached to grab the phone, I suddenly felt my forehead bathed in a cold sweat and my legs buckling beneath me. I grabbed on to the kitchen cabinet to steady myself but felt all the strength draining from my body. I fell to the floor.

The phone stopped ringing. "What the hell is happening to me?" I wondered, as a million thoughts began coursing through my brain.

Then, I remembered what a friend of mine, Dr. Mark Mostovych, had said to me just a few weeks earlier. He just happens to be a renowned cardiothoracic surgeon in Jacksonville, Florida, and his words came roaring back to me. "Oscar, you'd never believe how many people die on my operating table and they have no idea they're having a heart attack."

It couldn't be a heart attack, I thought. I hadn't even run that hard. "If you ever feel weird," I remember him saying, "don't hesitate; just call 911. If you're lucky, the worst that happens is you feel foolish for a false alarm."

I certainly didn't feel the classic symptoms depicted in the movies. No pain, no tingling in the arm, no clutching my chest; just an overwhelming sense of feeling seriously . . . "weird."

Had Mark not made his point so forcefully to me, I probably would have dismissed my fainting, cold sweat, and weak knees as mere exhaustion from my run and lack of sleep. I probably would've laid myself down on the couch until it passed, which would've been the last mistake I'd ever have the chance to make.

It's bizarre how, in moments of life and death, the sacred mixes with the mundane. *How much fun would pundits have with this?* I thought, darkly.

"United Airlines and its CEO, both on death's door."

"United gave Munoz a heart attack."

"Oh, and one more thing," I remembered Mark saying, "when you call 911, immediately tell them where you are, because you may not make it past the phone call."

That's a tad dramatic, I thought at the time.

Dismissive no longer, I crawled along the apartment floor and reached for the landline phone on the counter. I dialed 911 and relayed my location on the forty-eighth floor. Then it occurred to me. "I'd better unlock the door." So I kept crawling along the floor toward the entranceway, my legs refusing to help me. I reached up with my last ounce of strength and unlocked the dead bolt.

The very last thing I remember before losing consciousness was seeing the faces of EMTs—a woman followed by a man, both of Latino heritage—as they stepped over the pool of blood that was gushing from my smashed face; somewhere along the way I had hit my nose, hard. Then, it was "fade to black."

CHAPTER 5

IN LIMBO

On Saturday—the third day of my medically induced coma—the beeping and whirring of the various life-support machines in the ICU mingled with the sounds of college football playing on the television.

The USC Trojans—an alma mater for Cathy and me—were playing the Fighting Irish at Notre Dame Stadium, an annual fall classic that usually brings our family together for a celebratory weekend. This game marked a decidedly somber reunion—and not just because USC was getting killed on the field—as my family sat in a semicircle around my bed while I lay unconscious.

Cathy and I had tickets to the game, and we had been looking forward to taking a train to Notre Dame's campus and tailgating with a large group of USC's senior leaders, as well as our old gang of college friends. Cathy's brother, John Moulton, and his wife had flown in to Chicago a day earlier, and John was the first person to arrive at the hospital on Thursday, after he received the call from Cathy about what had happened.

The kids had channeled their grief and anxiety by decorating the place, trying to put a homespun touch to the antiseptic environs. USC pennants and regalia that were meant to decorate the pregame tailgate now festooned my hospital room.

Though visiting hours typically ended at 8:00 p.m., Cathy refused to leave my side until I woke from the coma, no matter how long that would be. The hospital staff kindly obliged. Kellie watched over Cathy as she maintained her vigil, while the other kids took shifts napping at my apartment nearby. They each had to try to carry on with their high school, college, and graduate school studies as best they could, while pitching in to help with whatever was needed, especially in calling all the relatives who hadn't heard the news yet.

When they walked into the rental unit on the first night, they could see the dried blood on the floor where the paramedics found me.

Over the next few days, the kids found creative ways to distract themselves: playing silly games and pranks on one another, making fast friends with the nurses and staff, entertaining the other patients (possibly annoying them), and creating funny Triller videos of themselves singing and dancing around. All this, they hoped, would cheer me up when I woke—all this, believing I *would* wake.

• • •

If the day of my heart attack was scary for my family, it was downright strange for my team back at United headquarters.

I had been a no-show for the scheduled breakfast interview meeting that morning. Next, I missed a meeting with a partner at Boston Consulting Group. Then, I never arrived at the long-awaited meeting with union leaders, without even a text, leaving everyone in an uncomfortable limbo: from the CFO candidate who was left waiting for me at a restaurant to the union bosses we'd gathered for the meeting to my new colleagues back at the office.

By lunchtime, Sonja was beginning to get seriously worried. After a few hours of wait and see, it was time to tell Kate Gebo, my chief of staff, and Brett Hart, then executive vice president and general counsel—now serving as president—that the CEO of United was missing.

In my first weeks, the four of us—Kate, Brett, Sonja, and I—had formed a tightly knit unit and, in turn, the three of them had assumed a kind of praetorian guardship, protecting my back. Our offices in the C-Suite were clustered, one next to the other, with Sonja's desk at the center.

Two weeks before the heart attack I had hired Kate as chief of staff from her role as head of corporate real estate, which was a position of central power within the company, responsible for negotiating contracts everywhere we operate, especially at airports where airlines fight tooth and nail for prime space.

That experience translated well into her new role because it meant she knew every inch of our global network like the back of her hand. More important, she knew the people of United better than anyone—from the power brokers in every airport authority and city where we operated, to every hub manager, to the newest hires at headquarters, whom she had generously taken under her wing.

Her stature within the company derived from something bigger than her title, though. Her exemplary and peripatetic career at the company offered a compelling example of the rich and varied opportunities that United offers.

Sonja and Kate had worked hard to keep track of me during my travels and now it looked like they had finally lost me.

Before their concerns could run too far out of control, however, Sonja received that call from Cathy, telling her that I had injured myself while running. With the crisis seemingly averted, Sonja went back to work as usual.

As she left the building for the evening, at around 7:30 p.m., Sonja's phone rang—an "unknown number."

"Hello," she answered.

"I'm calling about you-know-who," said a male voice on the other end, in an unsettling monotone. "He has had a heart attack and is at Northwestern." The call ended.

Sonja doubled back to the Willis Tower, trying Kate on her cell phone as she hurried. No answer. She called Brett. No answer. Then she tried Brett again, finally getting hold of him at dinner.

She began to tell him what just happened, but Brett cut her short. He told her to stay in the office and he would meet her there to discuss it in person.

Though United employees often pull long nights, by this time nearly all the floors were vacated, the offices cloaked in semidarkness. Sonja sat at her desk, which faces toward mine, nervously waiting until Brett arrived.

"Preternaturally cool," that's the best way I can describe what Brett's like, almost always cerebral and composed.

There was one occasion, however, during a visit to our maintenance hangar at Washington-Dulles, that a Tech Ops worker got a little too heated during a conversation with me. In fact, it got to the point where Brett thought seriously that he might need to physically put himself between me and an incoming shove.

Thankfully, we were able to reason with the guy, but I was glad to know Brett was behind me, all the same.

As executive vice president and general counsel for United, Brett was well known in Chicago's business world, plugged into the city's politics, and a respected leader within the city's Black community.

Brett proved to be the ultimate consigliere to me, the person in our C-Suite with a breadth of professional experience to help me frame issues in all the variety of contexts in which United operates—legal, political, cultural, reputational.

Raised in small-town Michigan, Brett grew up reading the history of lawyers who shaped the civil rights movement in America, and it sparked in him twin lifelong passions—for the law and social justice. While earning his law degree from the University of Chicago, he spent his time outside the lecture hall at the Mandel Legal Aid Clinic on the university's southside campus, providing free legal representation to the city's poorest, most vulnerable communities, even arguing before the Illinois Human Rights Commission.

That evening, standing in front of my empty office, Brett told Sonja to repeat what she had heard, verbatim.

For all his sangfroid, when Sonja told him the news, Brett—"Mr. Cool"—cringed, knowing that there couldn't be a worse time for United to lose yet another CEO. He told Sonja to go home and get some rest, it had been a long day.

Even now, we still have no idea to whom the voice on the other end of that anonymous call belonged or how that person could have known about my medical situation. I'd been admitted to the hospital as a John Doe. Thereafter, I used an alias to protect my privacy—Peter Hall, borrowing from the middle and last names of my daughter Jessica's new husband, Matt Hall.

While the United team searched for my whereabouts, my kids began receiving calls on their cell phones from reporters asking for comment. Obviously, the information had leaked. Was someone trying to help us? Hurt us? Brett and Kate had no clue.

Northwestern would launch a formal investigation into this curious case, at the request of its CEO, to find out how a patient's rights to HIPAA protections had been violated.

The mystery endures.

Brett's next move was to inform the chairman of the board, Henry Meyer, about the situation. Over the course of several conversations that evening, it was agreed that, to comply with the company's fiduciary responsibilities, a statement would be released to the media by midmorning the following day.

Both Brett and Henry understood the need for transparency but were also acutely aware that the news could send shares of United's stock tumbling and investor confidence cratering.

The press narrative wrote itself; United had become known in financial media circles as the "sick man" of the airline industry. Now, its CEO was knocking on death's door. The irony was almost too much.

The previous CEO had already left under adverse circumstances, and it was looking like they would need to find a third CEO in as many months. The optics of losing one CEO can be regarded as a misfortune, to paraphrase Oscar Wilde; to lose two begins to look like carelessness.

There was another elephant in the room that I imagine was on Brett's and Henry's minds as they worked through this process: I wasn't formally an employee yet.

So many things were happening all at once during my first weeks that I still hadn't finalized my employment contract by the time of the heart attack.

My lawyer had been pestering me about it. "Oscar, you better review the paperwork and sign it," he insisted, "at least for your own security. You never know what could happen." I had been so busy in those crowded first weeks that I simply hadn't gotten around to it. "What's the worst that could happen?" I joked—famous last words.

Brett was the obvious choice for Henry to name as CEO on an interim basis. It was not a role he had aspired to or anticipated; it would bring with it heavy responsibilities and a media glare that neither he nor his family had asked for, and yet he did it all the same. He held down the fort, taking flak and protecting my back when I was too weak to do so.

It wasn't the first time Brett had been my saving grace. It would prove far from the last.

• • •

By now, Cathy's brother, John Moulton, had interceded and connected with my United team. As a longtime partner at Deloitte, specializing in accounting and audit, John had deep experience working with the boards of large corporations, and he was well positioned to act as a go-between from the family to United, negotiating the fine line between family privacy and the responsibilities of a publicly traded company to be transparent.

My oldest daughter, Jessica, deputized herself into the role as the family's medical liaison to the doctors and nurses. I always say that the very best of my children's qualities they owe to their mother. But there are a few traits I notice in them, from time to time, that I recognize as, unmistakably, me. And Jessica's tenacity, her refusal to give up, no matter what, was something we shared as part of our bond as father and daughter. The epitome of an oldest child with a type A personality, Jessica decided she would take over the care strategy, at least from the family's perspective. She tried to help the staff in ways that endeared her to them, while also asking incessant questions, which probably didn't. When it was her shift to sit by my bedside through those early days, keeping Cathy company, she would spend the hours researching the intricacies of my condition.

As Saturday stretched into Sunday, then Monday, the family noticed that my right arm appeared swollen, distended. It felt cold to the touch, hard as plastic, dead.

Soon, the doctors concluded that I was experiencing acute compartment syndrome, a dangerous condition wherein pressure builds within the muscle tissue, often leading to a loss of limb or even sudden death. There wasn't even enough time to get me into an operating theater. Right there in my hospital room, while I was still in the coma, they immediately prepped me for emergency fasciotomy surgery, a procedure that involves cutting into the muscle, nerves, and tendons to relieve the pressure.

This triggered a whole new problem. Because I had been placed on anticoagulants, I immediately began bleeding uncontrollably in the room, nearly losing all the vital blood supply in my body. Massive blood transfusions were then administered, made more complicated by the fact that the blood would have to cycle through the ECMO machine that cleaned and oxygenated it.

More blood was transfused into my body, then went into the machine, then bled out again from area of my arm where the doctors were operating. This process continued until I was out of danger.

Ultimately, the surgery was successful, the bleeding slowed, and I stabilized.

I'm certainly glad that I was in a coma, sparing me the pain—and, also, that the family had been cleared out of the room.

Thanks to the immaculate skills of the surgeon, the arm was saved, and still looks relatively normal, though severely scarred. Shaking hands would remain painful for years afterward, something I'd do hundreds of times a day when visiting employees. The damaged nerves would send a snap of pain up my arm, and I'd mask my grimace with a smile.

By the seventh day, my vital signs had stabilized, and the medical team was ready to remove the ventilator and gradually bring me out of the coma. "Oscar," I heard a voice saying. "Oscar, can you open your eyes for me?"

I tried to speak, but my throat was swollen and painful. I couldn't wring the sounds out or move my mouth, which was blistered by sores and lesions from the tubes that had been stuck down my windpipe, and the Swan-Ganz catheter that had been inserted into my neck.

I blinked my eyes as they adjusted to the bright lights that created a halo effect around the figures standing over me. After a moment, I began to recognize the faces of my family. As I looked at each of them, holding one another tightly, tears in their eyes, I knew that I was the beneficiary of a miracle.

It was hard to believe that the last time all of us had been together was four and half weeks earlier at our home in Florida, as I walked Jessica down the aisle.

CHAPTER 6

KNOWLEDGE OF CONTRIBUTION

F riends and family had traveled from far and wide to be with us over Labor Day 2015, to celebrate Jessica's wedding to her fiancé, Matt, in the backyard of our family home, overlooking the beach, where we had made so many memories over the years.

When I walked into our family room and saw Jessica standing there in her wedding dress, alongside her bridesmaids, my heart skipped a beat. At once, I saw her for the remarkable, accomplished, poised woman she had become and for the little girl she would forever be in my eyes. I felt pangs of pride and nostalgia to see Kellie in her maid-of-honor dress, standing next to her big sister. And Kevin and Jack, suddenly so mature-looking in their suits. I knew from that moment on, nothing would ever be quite the same for our family.

Many more changes were swiftly on the way, but only Cathy and I knew of them as of yet.

Five days earlier, I had resigned from my job as president and chief operating officer of CSX, the Florida-based railroad company where I had worked the previous twelve years.

In two days, I would be boarding a flight to Chicago to start a new job as CEO of United, a job that would bring with it changes and challenges I could never have anticipated.

Against the setting sun, the newlyweds exchanged vows under the shade of an arbor that framed them and the ocean beyond.

During the cocktail hour, before the reception, as guests mingled with Cathy and the kids, I retreated to my small office inside the house. I nervously paced back and forth, adjusting my tie and rehearsing my father-of-the-bride speech under my breath. I scratched last-minute ideas into the margins of my notecards, all the while trying to ignore the incessant buzzing from my phone. Every other minute, my phone would vibrate again with an email or text message interrupting my train of thought.

I didn't need to check who was texting. I knew it was coming from the war room in Chicago.

If it were a movie, the scene would've made for a stark split-screen image. While I put the finishing touches on my speech—reflecting on the nature of commitment, embracing life's unpredictability, and emphasizing and waxing upon the importance of cherishing every moment—lawyers and corporate communications people were huddled around a conference table in the offices of a prominent Chicago law firm.

They were furiously writing press releases, talking points, and SEC filings in preparation for the announcement that I would be taking over as the new CEO of United when markets opened on Tuesday, after the holiday weekend.

The succession plan was a closely held secret, with precious few people aware of the lengthy process that led us to this moment—not the executive leadership team at United; not the employees, front line, or management; not the media or investor community; not even our kids were aware of the news that was about to drop.

During the long preamble to this moment, Cathy and I had talked many times about what we would decide to do if I were offered the top job at United.

"Whatever happens," Cathy would tell me each time, "just make sure you get your speech done for Jessica's wedding. Okay?"

I looked over the speech one more time, turned my phone to airplane mode (yes, the irony wasn't lost on me), and walked out to the reception.

I fulfilled my promise to Cathy, making it through my speech without losing my emotions entirely. As the reception extended late into the night, filling our home with life and warmth, the team in Chicago was also burning the midnight oil, preparing for an announcement that would end the high-stakes, behind-the-scenes corporate legal drama that had begun more than eight months prior when Brett Hart first told me that there was a problem at United.

• • •

Hillary Clinton, Jane Goodall, and Martha Stewart walk into a room . . .

No, it's not the setup for a joke, it's just another of the strange and interesting experiences that come with the job of airline CEO. A few years into my tenure, Marc Benioff, the founder and CEO of the cloud computing giant Salesforce—where I currently serve on the board—invited me to speak at an event hosted by *Time* magazine, which he had recently purchased.

Those three luminaries were but a few of the headliners at the event.

The greenroom that day was filled with such high-level dignitaries and VIPs, the famous and powerful, the great and the good . . . and me. With the star power in rooms like that, you'd think the CEO of an airline wouldn't be such a big draw. Yet, as I talked with one person, I noticed out of the corner of my eye a receiving line forming behind him. By this point in my tenure, I could guess what it was they wanted to chat with me about.

In TV studio greenrooms to golf courses, airport lounges to sports events, to simply walking down the street, there's never a shortage of people who will bend your ear, subtly making their way toward the subject they had in mind all along.

"Hey, Oscar, you should really think about flying from [fill in city] to [fill in favorite destination], and landing around [fill in ideal time]," is how it usually goes. "It would be a great route, Oscar. Think about it!"

You become used to such lobbying. Usually, it's harmless, so long as there's no quid pro quo.

Yet, at the end of January 2015, the Department of Justice alleged that United had engaged in precisely that kind of deal. The feds had begun serving subpoenas to senior executives, including my predecessor. Following this, I received a message from Brett Hart, urgently telling me to get in touch with him. Per my role as chair of the audit committee on UA's board, I needed to be one of the first to know what was unfolding.

I was in Southern California at the time for a "small" family gathering. Of course, when you belong to a Mexican American household of nine siblings, there's no such thing as a small family gathering.

We were throwing a housewarming party for our dad, Eduardo, to celebrate the new place we'd rented for him in Huntington Beach.

With all the rooms filled with the chaos of grandchildren, nieces, and nephews bouncing off the walls, my dad's favorite westerns playing loudly on the TV, and the din of my sisters cooking in the kitchen, I stepped outside and retreated to the quiet sanctuary of my rental car parked in the driveway so I could return the call to Brett.

The details were still coming into focus, but the main thrust was clear. Suspicions among the press and federal regulators had been raised by a twice-weekly flight between Newark Liberty Airport and Columbia, South Carolina, which just so happens to be very near the vacation home owned by the then chairman of the Port Authority of New York and New Jersey. The feds suspected that this flight, which the press would later dub the "Chairman's Flight," was a money loser for United and existed only to curry favor with the head of the Port Authority vis-à-vis some important capital projects that we currently had before his consideration—at the price of providing him with his very own direct flight to his vacation home.

I could scarcely believe my ears as Brett told me the news. I knew this would dominate the discussions at the next meeting of the board, which would be taking place a few days later in San Francisco.

Still stunned by what I'd heard, I stepped out of my rental car and began walking back up the driveway to the house. I paused for a moment and looked around at the beautiful neighborhood, the kids playing on the manicured lawns, parents pushing strollers, enjoying the golden hour of late afternoon.

And I thought back to the neighborhood where we were raised as kids. Though our parents moved us to the nicer Santa Ana area in later years, when I first immigrated to the United States at eight years old, we lived in Norwalk—a sometimes dangerous, always colorful community. We lived in a section of Norwalk referred to by locals as "One Ways" due to the narrow graffitied streets that guide traffic into single one-way-only lanes in and out of the area.

Though Huntington Beach and Santa Ana are only an hour's drive from the old neighborhood in Norwalk, my family had come a long way in just a single generation.

• • •

Brett had already briefed Henry Meyer, our board chair, about DOJ's investigation into United's executives. The information would remain privileged until Brett could inform the board of the situation when we convened in early February 2015 in San Francisco.

The words "banker" and "beloved" aren't often used in the same sentence or applied to the same person. But in Henry they cohered. He was, indeed, well loved as the longtime CEO of KeyBank—a Cleveland institution. Falstaffian in both appearance and demeanor, Henry epitomized midwestern warmth, kindness, and an old-fashioned business ethic: you knew his word was his bond.

His good nature and evident people skills helped him maintain unity on the board as we tried to unite the warring factions of the merged company.

I give enormous credit to Henry's leadership, especially in that difficult time. He immediately made it clear that United wouldn't circle the wagons and stonewall an investigation. Instead, he proactively launched an internal investigation of our own to determine who in senior leadership knew about this situation and what was to be done. The board had to conduct its own independent investigation precisely because it had no knowledge or insight into the matter—until the government began issuing subpoenas, that is.

The responsibility for deciding if flights should be added or removed from our schedule belongs to the senior leaders in network planning and management. They report, ultimately, to the C-Suite and the CEO. These day-to-day decisions simply don't rise to the level of the board. That's why no members of the board were targeted by the investigation. We did not create the problem, but it would be our responsibility to address it.

If the allegations were true, the board's task would be to determine— as the famous Watergate-era saying goes—who knew what and when did they know it.

Since Brett had not been issued a subpoena, and due to his role as general counsel, he was free to act as a consigliere to us as we worked our way through the gathering shitstorm.

Brett had already taken immediate steps to engage a prominent Chicago-based lawyer, Craig Martin, who had leapt into action and took receipt of the subpoenas. Craig would serve as an entirely independent counsel, not representing United but rather exclusively advising the board.

Following Craig's legal advice, we created a special subcommittee to handle the matter, comprised of four directors: Henry; John Walker, another accomplished CEO in his own right; David Vitale, a prominent business and civic leader in Chicago; and myself. This subcommittee would be responsible for reviewing the work of Craig's team and playing the role of liaison between his independent investigation, DOJ, and the broader United board.

This process would engage us for the next seven months, from February to August, as we became fully versed in the granular details. We needed to be prepared to make decisions on what steps the company should take in response should indictments be handed down.

Our committee would conduct no fewer than thirty-five sessions with Craig's team, receiving updates to its internal investigation, in addition to several one-on-ones with Craig himself. At my request, he even came down to Jacksonville, lugging several boxes of materials with him. I'll never forget sitting with him in my office at CSX, going through all that the DOJ had compiled regarding the matter.

At a certain point in those first few months, Henry began the quiet process of potential succession planning, if indeed any action would have to be taken against the sitting CEO. Henry gave me a call and took my temperature about being considered for the job, should that become necessary.

I told him I was humbled and honored but, nevertheless, dismissed the possibility outright. I had too many irons in the fire at my current employer, CSX—it was where my heart was, and it was where I saw my future. Besides, such discussion was premature; we were still nowhere close to reaching a decision with respect to the fate of any UA executives.

Though I left it unsaid with him, Henry was fully aware of the fact that I had just become president of CSX the previous year, in 2014, and I was the odds-on favorite to take over the railroad when my boss and mentor, Michael Ward, eventually retired.

For his part, Michael Ward knew that something iffy was going on at United and that my duties on the board were consuming an unusually large amount of my attention. While I was bound by certain confidentialities, I explained as a courtesy to Michael that over the next few months my office door might be closed for long stretches of the day and that my attention might be focused elsewhere than on CSX.

Michael said he understood, but he took that moment to remind me of a few facts of life, preemptively.

Airlines were flying low, and railroads were flying high—so to speak—something I was well aware of. Even during a period of enormous profitability and growth for the industry, US airlines still garnered only razor-thin profit margins compared to the railroad business. For example, in 2015, CSX routinely expected roughly 30 percent profit margins. The operating margins for US airlines, in contrast, were as thin as single digits to low teens.

Moreover, as president of the railroad, I was likely to emerge as the heir apparent at CSX. If I suddenly left, it would probably be damaging to the company as well as to Michael's legacy.

As spring turned into summer, and the investigation continued to heat up, Henry called me once again. "Oscar," he said, "we've engaged a search firm in the event we will need to name a new CEO. I know that you are married to CSX, but your name keeps floating to the top of the short list. No promises, obviously," he caveated, "but if you want your name considered, I need to know now."

This time, I hesitated.

Henry knew of my loyalty to the team at CSX and to Michael in particular. I had been clear in my refusal the first time.

Nevertheless, he had called again. I knew Henry too well to assume this gesture was made out of courtesy, or as simply a backup plan. Henry was too meticulous, and he would surely be aware that, whoever got the job, his selection process would meet with strictest scrutiny from the full board, as well as investors, the media, and regulators.

And yet he had still felt it necessary to reach out a second time.

I had to ask myself, "Why?" I thought I had a hunch based on a conversation that had taken place at that San Francisco board meeting back in February, just days after I had learned of the investigation.

At welcoming drinks on the first evening, Walter Isaacson, famed public intellectual and fellow UA board member, asked for a quick word. We stepped into a quiet area of the lobby and were joined by several other board members. We spoke in hushed tones.

"Oscar," Walter said, leaning in, speaking sotto voce in his Louisiana twang, "we are concerned where the company is going. You seem to be one of the few people whom management *actually listens* to, because you have an operational background, as opposed to some of us who don't have the expertise that you do."

Such attempts at flattery and self-deprecation are part of Walter's southern manners and sense of humor, but they're belied by a résumé that is nearly as lengthy as some of his heaviest tomes.

When Walter Isaacson speaks, you listen.

Did I think Walter, Henry, and the other board members were right?

Many people have asked me to help them weigh a difficult career choice over the years. I've had the privilege of being interviewed and hired by some extraordinary leaders, and I've been honored to hire even more.

Each time I sit across from someone, whether in terms of a formal interview or just friendly advice, I ask them: "How well do you know yourself?"

The person will then launch into a rehearsed speech. "No," I'll interject, "really, do you know yourself to the point you can tell me what you do well and what you don't do well?"

Take a hard look at yourself, I'll suggest. Ascertain a practical understanding of the demands of the role you are considering and determine whether you have the right skills to meet them, a concept I refer to as "Knowledge of Contribution."

Do you like the people you might be working with? Do you share common values and mission? Does the company need the skills you possess? If you got the job, would you be able to contribute something important, over and above what another person might?

I've seen too many aspiring young professionals get their progress dashed on the shoals of their own ambitions, having accepted a job for which their talents and skills didn't correspond. I've often seen some of the smartest people leave an interview with me crestfallen, as if they'd failed somehow to impress me. That's, of course, not the case at all. It's simply that their potential contributions weren't what the organization needed at that moment.

The ability to walk away from an opportunity because it's not right for you is precisely what sets the most successful people I've worked with apart from the rest. It's equally important to be able to recognize where your contributions might make a difference—even if it leads you down a path you didn't expect.

During Henry's second phone call, the career advice I'd given to others was now something I'd need to listen to myself. And it wasn't easy. I had to ask myself, seriously, if I was declining an opportunity that I might be right for simply because I was so focused on the CSX role. Remaining there, potentially succeeding Michael as CEO, was certainly the easier, smarter path for me career-wise. But were my responsibilities only to myself?

On this second call, I told Henry to keep my name on the list, still not really believing that anything would come of it. Yet I also felt my loyalties beginning to divide themselves—United vs. CSX.

My loyalty to Michael was based on the fact that he had taken a big risk by hiring me in 2003. Back then, Michael was taking over a struggling railroad. The company had already had ten chief operating officers in as many years.

CSX routinely ranked at the bottom of US railroads for operational efficiency, safety, and profitability. Morale among employees had plummeted and union tensions were spiking over multiple issues, not the least being a perceived lack of regard for employees' safety and well-being on the job. All of it was worsened by a previous failure to integrate a smaller rail company, Conrail, that CSX had bought—rather expensively.

Though CSX's problems in 2003 were never as dire as United's, circa 2015, if you're thinking that some of this has a déjà vu quality to it, you're not wrong.

Determined to turn the railroad around, Michael began assembling an all-star team to help him do it.

At that time, I was busy raising a very young family in Mendham, New Jersey, and working as CFO of consumer services at AT&T, which included what was then the highly lucrative long-distance phone business (something a younger reader may have to look up on Wikipedia). I had joined AT&T with the expectation that I would help take that division of the company public. However, the rise of the internet and sudden ubiquity of email had completely disrupted that business model. In the process, it dashed our plans to take the business public and for me to become CFO of a major publicly traded entity. On the upside, this development left me with the contractual option to become a free agent and look for new opportunities.

At forty-two years old, I was at a crossroads and my phone started ringing with queries from headhunters. In the months that followed, it began looking increasingly likely that I would land a prestigious job at a large financial institution, which was conveniently headquartered in nearby Manhattan.

That's when another headhunter reached out to me and extended an invitation to meet the new chief executive of CSX in Florida. "What's CSX?" I replied.

My next question probably was, "And why are you calling me?" After all, I knew next to nothing about railroads.

"Just come down for a meeting . . . and maybe some golf," the CSX headhunter insisted. I looked out the window at the harsh winter conditions of the Northeast and felt the proposition hard to argue against. So, a few days later, I found myself in Michael Ward's office.

I didn't want to waste his time. After all, I didn't see how I would fit into the culture, adjust to living in a new community, and compete in an industry I knew little about. Nonetheless, I took the meeting. Perhaps I did so because, even at that stage in my career, I was loath to turn down job offers, having been raised never to take an opportunity for granted.

• • •

I was born in Mexico and raised by my maternal grandmother—Mama Josefina, I called her.

My mother, Francisca—still in her early twenties—had left for Los Angeles when I was an infant so she could earn more money to send back to us in Mexico. In fact, until I was reunited with my mom in the States, I believed Mama Josefina was my true mother.

My earliest memories are of walking by my grandmother's side, her coarsened hand clasping mine, as we would travel the countryside, just the two of us, by train or by bus, from village to village, prevailing on the kindness of friends and family—as we had no home to call our own. In the culture I grew up in, the concept of "La Familia" is by no means exclusive to the bond between blood relatives. When I was growing up, every older person was a "tio" or "tia" (uncle or aunt), and I referred to so many people as cousins who, biologically speaking, were not.

This powerful spirit of inclusion, the bond of La Familia, opened doors for us as we made our way from one place to another, from one relative or distant family acquaintance to the next. And we were happy to earn our keep for as long as we were welcome under someone's roof, hoping that one day we would be welcomed in America.

Eventually, that day arrived and my uncle—Humberto Camacho, or Tio Beto—helped us make the journey north. I would settle in the Los Angeles area, with my mother and her new family, including her husband, Eduardo.

Mama Josefina found stable work as a housekeeper at a Las Vegas hotel chain. She retired at the tender age of eighty-six, after nearly two decades. I would later learn—because she would never tell anyone—that in the last few years on the job arthritis had caused the bones in her right ankle to fuse, making it incredibly painful just to walk, much less work. But she never complained.

She was my role model. For the rest of my career, no matter how great the challenge or how difficult the circumstance, I could always draw inspiration from her example, as well as humility from the knowledge that the worst day in my job was far, far easier than the best day in hers.

Even as I started to succeed in my career, she could never quite understand just what it was that I did for a living. One day, still in my thirties, I excitedly told her that I had been promoted to become CFO of a division within the Coca-Cola Company. "What does that mean?" she asked—again, in Spanish—seeming confused and a little sad for me when I tried to explain the role. In her family and within our heritage it's the workers—the people who make the product and deliver it—who are respected and praised. She worried that I might not be too bright if all I did was sit in an office, pushing papers around a desk.

I could only imagine what she would say if she knew I was thinking about turning down the cushy job offers I had in front me. "If they offer you a job, whatever it is, take it!" I could hear her urge in Spanish.

"After all, you can never be sure you'll be offered another job again." My blue-collar adoptive dad, Eduardo, my eight brothers and sisters, and the friends I hung out with as a kid while growing up in our South Central LA neighborhood—the "One Ways"—would have surely agreed.

• • •

Back at my interview at CSX, as Michael and I broke the ice, it seemed—at first glance—that the two of us were worlds apart.

I soon came to appreciate that while we came from very different places and cultures—he from the working-class environs of the East Coast, and I from the Mexican immigrant culture of Los Angeles—we shared common values and perspectives.

An interview that was scheduled for an hour turned into several, eventually consuming the whole afternoon.

Then, it was dinner and drinks, where he told me about how he intended to take this sleepy railroad company and turn it into an industry leader. His plan was to rebuild morale by focusing on safety as the first step toward reestablishing the trust of employees. This, he believed, would then lead to greater operational consistency and durable profits.

We agreed on the types of leaders he was looking to hire and how to rebuild the company's internal culture.

As one Jack Daniel's turned into another over dinner, slowly but surely, I came to see how I could play a role in his turnaround strategy, and I felt increasingly excited to be getting in on the ground floor.

Being practical at this point, I tapped on the brakes and told him that I was strongly considering a job in New York. If that opportunity worked out, it would be easier for my family, I explained, and less off the beaten track, so to speak, career-wise. Taking this railroad job still felt like a risky bet, by comparison.

Michael reduced a complicated decision matrix into a succinct choice.

Memory fades, but I recollect Michael telling me, "Look, Oscar, you can take that job in New York, and they'll offer more money."

He leaned over the table, gesturing with his glass of whiskey to emphasize his point. "On the other hand, if you were here at CSX, I would rely on you to actually help me run this corporation."

He was right. If I took the job offer with a big-name financial institution, I would be bound by a narrow remit and would need to stay in my lane. I would be a lieutenant, carrying out someone else's strategy, rather than a top general helping to devise one.

I needed to ask myself the hard questions, to ascertain my knowledge of contribution.

I had enough confidence in myself to see that CSX could use someone with my financial and operational skill set. I had humility enough to admit that there were any number of other candidates who could slide into the New York role and do just as well, perhaps better. I liked Michael and some of his key leaders, and I was really impressed with the finance team as I got to meet them over the next couple of visits to HQ. I could see us working well together—even our competitive styles would be an advantage, making us constantly challenge one another to perform at our best. Above all, I felt my contributions would be valued more at CSX than they would be at a traditional financial institution.

Michael was offering me a different path than the one I had envisioned, an opportunity to make this job my own and to help him build something new. In any case, it would be an adventure, a "track" less taken. Add to that, when the formal offer from Michael arrived, I discovered that he had expanded my role beyond the normal responsibilities of a CFO, to include technology, procurement, and strategic planning.

I couldn't pass it up.

I made a leap of faith, relocated my family to Florida, and over the next twelve years Michael and the team we assembled took a once low-profile stock and turned it into a Cinderella story on Wall Street, a darling of the financial news media.

We focused on the fundamentals: improving operations and managing revenue growth in a vastly different manner, allowing us to leverage our network and service to build an impressive top-line trajectory. Meanwhile, we worked to cut out many of the pain points that demoralized frontline workers. We elevated safety and rebuilt a culture that respected the workers who do the hard, physical labor that powers our industry. Or, as Mama Josefina would say, "the ones who do the work and deliver it."

Our railroad team delivered a decade of excellent operational performance, boosting operating income by nearly 600 percent, earning CSX recognition on the list of Most Honored Companies by *Institutional Investor* magazine, and establishing it as the premier freight operator in North America.

I learned how to work with a large, unionized, distributed workforce and to translate complex financial strategy into a game plan that could simultaneously win the hearts and minds of our investors, the communities we operated in, and also our frontline employees—skills that I never would have gained in the cloistered offices of a Manhattan-based firm.

As one success begat another, I began to see the sketches of a "turnaround playbook" taking shape in my mind. Twelve years later, that playbook had filled out, containing all that I had learned from Michael and my colleagues.

By January 2015, I was looking forward to the very real prospect of taking over from Michael and deploying that playbook as CEO. Except, CSX didn't need a turnaround anymore. We'd been there; done that.

I felt like I still had the energy in me for another big corporate turnaround. CSX didn't need one, but United certainly did.

By mid-2015, the United investigation was reaching its terminus and Craig Martin's firm was ready to present the results of its monthslong independent investigation to the special committee—Henry, John Walker, David Vitale, and myself. It would now be our responsibility to review the findings and make recommendations to the wider board concerning the fate of the executives involved, including the current CEO.

Once we had this information in hand, we had to act quickly. Soon, the government would begin holding grand jury interviews with key United personnel, and it would be vastly preferable if the board had already made decisions regarding the future employment of individuals under question.

Henry called for a meeting, and I packed a bag for Chicago.

CHAPTER 7

SUCCESSION

F ew cities are more stunning upon final descent than Chicago in the summertime. The inviting blue-green waters of Lake Michigan, ringed by miles of unobstructed shoreline, welcome you as you fly above the peaks of skyscrapers and then the neighborhoods beyond them.

I glanced out the airplane window as we passed over the beaches that stretched into the hazy distance. They were packed with people enjoying one of the last remaining summer weekends. The harbor teemed with racing boats, their white sails mixing with the white caps of the water.

Must be a very pleasant place to live, I caught myself musing.

My car pulled up to the curb in front of the high-rise office tower where Craig Martin's firm was located, just a few blocks away from United's headquarters at the Willis Tower. It was better, Henry had determined, to hold these sensitive meetings in private, away from United's offices, to limit rumors among staff and prevent leaks to the press.

As I opened the car door to get out, I was hit with a wall of humid midwestern summer air. Once I reached the conference room upstairs, I found that the atmosphere was equally heated.

While we had many items on the agenda for that day, our mandate was straightforward: protect United and the brand. Difficult, even painful, decisions would have to be made regarding some of the individuals allegedly involved, but we had to make it clear that we were determined to put our house in order, or else the feds would do it for us.

By midday Saturday, August 8, 2015, the agenda moved toward the topic of CEO succession, at which point Henry called for a quick break. He took me aside and discreetly told me it would be best if I absented myself from the meeting once it reconvened.

He didn't show his cards or say anything explicit to me, but I fully understood; given that I was a potential candidate to take over, I should have no part in deciding to remove a predecessor, should that come to pass.

Soon, the meeting resumed, and the conference room doors closed, with me on the other side. One of Craig's associates showed me to the foyer, where I could make myself comfortable while I waited. Unable to sit still, I paced the shiny marble floor, lost in thought, the silence broken only when someone would occasionally ask if I needed anything.

I gazed out the floor-to-ceiling windows, taking in the view to the north, toward the obsidian-looking obelisk skyscraper formerly known as the Hancock Building. The city hummed with life and felt more vital, more vibrant, than the laid-back beach community vibes of Ponte Vedra. The notion of living here began to grow on me.

In a strange bit of irony, Craig's offices looked down on my future apartment building that stood across the street, where the drama of my heart attack would play out. But all that was in the future.

The meeting adjourned and, despite the stifling heat, my board colleague John Walker and I decided to take a leisurely stroll back to our hotel.

"So," John said, casually, after we'd walked a few blocks, "how are you thinking about all this?"

John didn't betray anything that had been discussed during their private session. He didn't have to. Even without a wisp of breeze on that dog day afternoon, I knew which way the wind was blowing at United.

The lawyers representing UA executives who were facing legal jeopardy had informed Craig that their clients planned to plead the Fifth in their upcoming testimonies to the federal grand jury, including the then CEO. That was their right, as it is for every American. However, the optics would have made their positions untenable at the company, which meant the need for a new chief executive was now inevitable and immediate.

I began to sense that Henry would be calling me for a third and final time. I would need to have an answer ready.

Cathy had joined me on the trip to Chicago, as did our son Kevin and a friend of his. As we enjoyed the city for the weekend, my mind mulled the pros and cons between staying at CSX and taking the leap to United—if Henry should make the offer, that is.

I still have the pictures we took of us that weekend. There's one of us lying underneath the *Cloud Gate* sculpture—affectionately nicknamed "The Bean"—a giant teardrop of mirror-smooth steel that reflects the cityscape and the people surrounding it. Another photo shows us enjoying a drink at one of the many cafés that line the then newly constructed Riverwalk, which follows the path of the Chicago River as it snakes its way through the canyon of glassy skyscrapers downtown.

Once a heavily trafficked and polluted industrial waterway, the river had been cleaned up and transformed in recent years to emerge as a second recreational frontier for the city, rivaling even the lakefront in its popularity.

In the early 1900s, ambitious city planners had pulled off an engineering marvel, reversing the flow of the river, utilizing a series of locks and dams, so it emptied into inland canals rather than into Lake Michigan.

It was another staggering feat of genius that helped the city rise from the ashes of the Great Chicago Fire of 1871, leading to its reemergence as a city of global significance—a "Paris on the Prairie"—as envisioned by the architect Daniel Burnham in his 1909 Plan of Chicago.

"Make no little plans," he had said in defense of his grand designs. "They have no magic to stir men's blood and probably will not themselves be realized."

The course of life, unlike the direction of the river, cannot be engineered to flow backward, any more than—as Heraclitus once said—a person can step into the same river twice; it is not the same river, and you are not the same person.

I had to consider the possibility that the time for me at CSX had come, and it had passed.

I began interrogating myself, questioning my motivations for staying at CSX—assessing my "knowledge of contribution." The opportunity to take the baton from my mentor, Michael, in order to lead a team I had helped develop and to carry it forward was a profoundly fulfilling prospect.

United, on the other hand, was a clean canvas on which I could map a big, bold, ambitious turnaround agenda. "Make no little plans," indeed.

I talked with Cathy about what was weighing on me. In the end, she always had a knack for bringing me back down to earth, to remind me of my most important jobs, as a spouse and a dad. "Just be ready for Jessica's wedding," she repeated.

Not long after we returned home to Ponte Vedra from Chicago, Henry called and offered me the job at United. With the completion of Craig's report and the recommendations of our subcommittee in hand, the board had a fiduciary duty to inform shareholders and act, exiting the sitting CEO and announcing a new one at the same time.

He could allow me a week to make my decision, but no longer.

With only a few days left to decide, I was taking a contemplative walk on the beach when my cell phone rang. It was Walter Isaacson.

I assumed this phone call would be a sequel to our private talk that took place at the board meeting in February. The first one he framed as an appeal to me, on the board's behalf, then, deeply concerned about what the company had become. The second time, he framed it as a challenge to me personally; now, he was cautiously optimistic about what the airline might become, the reputation we might regain, if led by someone with the persistence and "street cred" to address the core challenges and also to relate them to the broader issues that roiled society then, many of which roil us still.

Like many large corporations, we struggled to unite fractious employees, deal with unions against the backdrop of disruptive changes that were taking place within the American labor movement, address racial and gender inequalities in the workplace, and face up to our role in arresting climate change and carbon emissions, among many other pressing issues.

United's global reach and influence, the unique role we play in so many countries and communities, meant we had an unparalleled opportunity to model a "new face of capitalism," as Walter put it to me that day to prove that a company can not only be profitable while principled but in fact can achieve greater profitability precisely when it hews doggedly to its principles.

Both consumers and employees saw the turmoil of the times and wished they could patronize or work for companies that were doing something to address them, persistently and ethically, not through worthily written public statements but through actions. Yet United, like most peer companies, had shown a reluctance to embrace this role.

Edelman, the communications firm, annually produced a "Trust Barometer"—a detailed study that gauges the changing attitudes held by different segments of the global population with respect to the credibility of traditional institutions, including the government and elected officials, business leaders and CEOs, as well as the media.

Corporations routinely ranked lowest in trust levels in those days, a position that has since improved precisely because they have begun to enlarge their sense of social responsibility, practicing a new version of "stakeholder capitalism," as my colleagues at the Business Roundtable have articulated the idea.

My experience at CSX provided a precursor to this point. For example, before Michael and I began working together, heavily investing in workers' experience and well-being was considered by Wall Street as "nice to have." Bucking that conventional wisdom, we made it a priority, and it became the basis of our turnaround success. Our emphasis on winning back the trust of employees at the railroad—not something that easily computes into a company's EBITDA (earnings before interest, taxes, depreciation, and amortization)—was the bedrock principle that led the way to soaring profits.

Demonstrating respect for frontline employees was a lesson as rooted in my life's experience as it was for my boss Michael. It was a lesson I learned from my dad, Eduardo. Back when I was a kid in junior high, on days during the summer when I was out of school and wasn't surfing—which weren't many—my dad would drive me in our mobile home to the supermarket where he worked as a meat cutter. I would help him out, sweeping floors or moving boxes—whatever he needed.

Even more lessons could be learned from how Mama Josefina worked and lived her life. When she finally retired from the housekeeping department of that Las Vegas hotel, her work friends threw a retirement party for her and invited me to come. I was still at the start of my career. I expected to find just a small gathering, maybe a cake and a few elderly ladies sipping coffee in a break room. To my utter surprise, I arrived to discover the hotel's management had granted the use of the entire main ballroom so they could fit everyone who showed up. I got to hear her colleagues, in impromptu speeches and toasts, describe her dedication and hard work. And I was impressed that her bosses in management had taken the effort—and expense—to honor the contributions she had made to the company by virtue of her sustained labor. From coworkers to the bosses in hotel management, the new hires as well as the old guard, everyone wanted to pay their respects to this woman—small in stature but towering in her resilience—who was always there for them and never missed a day of work.

I also learned important lessons from my mom's brother, Tio Beto, who helped us reach the United States by leveraging his union connections. He had become famous as president of the United Electrical, Radio and Machine Workers of America (UE), a democratic national union that counted tens of thousands of manufacturing workers in its membership roll. He was the first US union leader to build alliances with the labor movement in Mexico, a vital cultural bridge that endures to this day. He was also the first to build bridges between the Latino and African American communities, which had often been hostile toward each other, especially in Los Angeles, founding the Latino Coalition Against Apartheid.

He instructed his members in the art of courage, standing shoulder to shoulder with them as they braved police intimidation and threats from angry anti-union organizers across the country. He taught people how to organize, speak up for themselves, and hold their ground against strike-breakers armed with chains, baseball bats, and knives. He didn't flinch when faced with violence by cops and hired guns who didn't think the people for whom Tio Beto cared should enjoy the same dignity of work as anybody else.

As I considered my own knowledge of contributions, I was sure that my perspective, shaped by this background, would provide a basis upon which to rebuild our relationship with United's unions, which had severely deteriorated in previous years. Only a few months earlier, at an annual shareholders meeting, UA's management abruptly shut down union reps, cutting them off as they were communicating their concerns, making a flagrant display of disrespect to their membership—our colleagues.

As the only person of color serving on the United board at that time, I also could speak authentically to employees about—finally—building a more diverse and inclusive culture. I had always envisioned what might result if we could prioritize diversity and gender equity—framing the issue not as a matter of kind conscientiousness but rather as a matter of competitive advantage. If I took the job, I would focus on building pipelines of talent development that would create a more representative and inclusive company, at all levels, especially at the top, and therefore a more competitive airline.

Finally, I was acutely aware that I had worked in two industries with massive carbon footprints. At CSX, moving coal generated nearly 20 percent of revenue, and United burned billions of gallons of fossil fuels every year. As the father of young adults looking to begin families of their own, if I took the job at United, I would dedicate myself as an evangelist for the gospel of going green.

With Henry's deadline for an answer approaching, I called my longtime friend and former boss at US West, Sol Trujillo, a prolific CEO and global business leader with a career spanning three continents and at least as many industries—telecommunications, tech, and media. Sol and I had reconnected when he founded an organization called the Latino Donor Collaborative (LDC), a think tank that supports research into the economic status of the US Latino cohort. Our goal was to deploy that data to influence political leaders, the media, and the largest capital allocators in our society so they will recognize the economic and cultural power of US Latinos and begin to make decisions reflecting it.

Sol, never one to mince words, didn't hide his shock that I was even entertaining the possibility of turning down the United job. He had built the LDC, as well as started the annual L'ATTITUDE conference, the largest gathering of Latino business leaders in the country, precisely so we could all have a platform to advance the ideals we cared about. The CEO of an iconic American company provided one hell of a platform—and would mean there would be at least one Latino leading a Fortune 100 company.

"I've turned down a CEO job in the past," Sol explained to me, with an unusual touch of melancholy in his voice. "Let me tell you," he said, "regret is a hard pill to swallow." I knew he was right, and I couldn't bear the thought of resuming my seat on the board and constantly swallowing my regret.

My mind was made up. I felt I owed it to Michael to tell him about my decision, face-to-face. On Monday morning, August 31, 2015, I stepped into Michael's office, twelve years after I had first sat down with him for an interview.

I told him that the situation at United had accelerated and they asked me once again to take the CEO job, and I had finally accepted. My last day at CSX would be that Friday; I would stay in Jacksonville through the Labor Day weekend, to celebrate my daughter's wedding. My first day at United would be that following Tuesday. I apologized for the timing—so close to the CSX board's decision regarding Michael's successor—but events were dictating things, not me. I thanked him for the faith he had placed in me, the support he'd given me, and the friendship between us that I hoped would continue.

Michael took the news as one would expect, maybe even worse. He accepted my decision but told me that I would have to personally tell every member of our team that I was leaving—he wouldn't do it for me. I completely understood, I told him—I would never leave without putting things to rights.

I couldn't blame him for the hard feelings. I packed up my office and left the CSX offices for the final time.

Later that day, I received a call from Megan McCarthy, managing director of global communications for United, whom Brett had quietly let into the secret of what was in the offing.

In order to maintain that secrecy, she had engaged a PR firm, rather than her corporate communications team, to help me craft my introductory letter to employees. She emailed its final product to me, and I gave it a quick read-through.

Uh-oh, I thought to myself.

With this chance to make a first impression, I wanted to telegraph to employees my lofty ambitions, appealing to their optimism and acknowledging their well-earned cynicism. I wanted to convey to my new colleagues that this time would be different, that I would be a different kind of leader from what had come before me. But in the back of my mind, I kept hearing the lyrics from one of my favorite songs, "Won't Get Fooled Again" by the Who: Meet the new boss, same as the old boss . . .

That's exactly what employees would take from this industry-standard, boilerplate PR statement. It was a *Pravda*-like, sanitized version of the reality facing our airline. It glossed over the arduous journey that had led us to this fork in the road, admitting no mistakes and acknowledging none of the pain and frustration felt by so many who had become alienated by our past failures.

I knew this note would drop into inboxes with a thud.

"DELETE DOCUMENT." I sat down at my desk in the office at our home and came up with my own draft, one that came from the heart, and sent it to Walter Isaacson for his assistance and to Megan for her review.

At first, she was concerned, since it rang such a different tone than previous letters—conversational, informal, friendly—which I took as a compliment.

Over the next week, the three of us would hone it further.

Meanwhile, at Craig's offices in Chicago, the war room was humming to life, with select individuals from key departments brought into the circle of knowledge, including government affairs, investor relations, marketing, and employee communications. These departments had to know which hymnal to sing from, relaying a clear and consistent message to their stakeholders when the news was released.

The investor relations website as well as the employee intranet would have to be updated. Even the preflight safety video, which would play on hundreds of thousands of monitors on our aircraft the next morning, would need editing, because it featured my predecessor.

SEC filings, employee communications, media strategy, what we planned to say when we informed the executive leadership—everything had to click into place simultaneously by Tuesday morning when we would inform United's executive team of the change in leadership. The situation reminded me of the quote from John Adams: "thirteen clocks made to strike at once."

As Walter, Megan, and I batted various drafts, redrafts, and red-lined revisions back and forth, I was also working on my speech for Jessica's wedding.

• • •

The day after the wedding, the backyard was still a glorious mess from the reception party. The family and I waved goodbye to the newlyweds, Jessica and Matt, as they drove away from our home to the airport to begin their honeymoon.

The next day, Labor Day, I also arrived at the airport—bleary eyed from the celebration and the joyous tears—and boarded a flight to Chicago.

I wanted to take advantage of the fact that this would be the last time I would be able to fly our airline anonymously, with no one to put a nice polish on the service just for my benefit, and I wanted to note everything. It was a pretty lousy flight and, therefore, a perfect way to begin my tenure.

During my first weeks, I would ask colleagues, "What are the top ten dumbest things that we do?" an exercise that began with this flight. I fired up my iPad and created a list titled "What's Wrong?" and ticked off the items so far.

To start off, the aircraft was one of the older, smaller fifty-seaters, which meant it belonged to one of United's regional partners, not our "mainline service," and therefore not operated by UA employees. A flight might be operated by Mesa Airlines, Republic Airways, or SkyWest Airlines, but the ticket would say "United Express." While I appreciated the distinction, I knew most customers didn't. We were the ones who sold the ticket, and we were going to take the ride—and accept the credit and the blame.

I shuffled through the narrow single-aisle plane, stooping down in the cramped confines, tripping over carry-ons that were spilling out from underneath the seats, finally squeezing myself into 12A.

I had taken this flight before during my tenure on the board, but only occasionally. A business commuter who flies the route at least once a week for work would surely choose a different airline that operated larger, more comfortable aircraft, with the ability to offer upgrades. That's how we were losing loyal business travelers to our competitors on routes throughout our network.

After a short taxi to the runway, air traffic control held us on the tarmac, delaying departure; we'd be halted again on the tarmac in Chicago to wait for a gate to become available.

As the wait time stretched on, my list of dumb things kept growing, already exceeding ten items.

The coffee was bad, the food options limited for a nearly three-hour flight, which stretched longer because of the delays.

Then, I noticed something that was going right: the outstanding service of the flight attendant.

As the lights for the call button blinked up and down the aisle, with the passengers becoming increasingly weary and frustrated, I noticed how she responded to each person—caringly, enthusiastically, looking people in the eye and never losing her disarming smile.

When we finally got airborne, and things calmed down a bit, I decided to start my listening tour a bit early. I ambled toward the galley and said hello to her. Jenna was her name if I recall correctly—and I hope I do. With a long tenure in the industry, she clearly had seen it all and wasn't frazzled in the slightest by the extra demands on her service that afternoon.

"I'm sorry you have to deal with all of this today," I offered. She shrugged; I could tell she wasn't the type to complain, that she valued the job and took pride in her ability to solve people's problems, to win them over.

She had no idea who I was—just another passenger, unusually interested in how she felt about her work. After a few minutes of chatting, another call button rang, and she went to answer it.

Though Jenna worked for the regional airline, I knew our customers assumed she was a United employee. United received the most DOT customer service complaints per enplanement of any major carrier in 2014, with low employee morale the principal reason. If I could get at least five thousand Jennas working together—matching her resilience and spirit—and put them in a position to succeed, *Well, we might be able to make this airline work*, I thought to myself.

Returning to my seat, I retrieved my list of "What's Wrong?"

I drew a column next to it and began a second list, titled "What's Right?"

"Our people," I wrote at the top.

At the end of the day—however much automation we might introduce—we are in the people business. Our frontline employees are the face of the franchise, and they are what you remember most about flying with us—for good or ill.

We needed to invest in our service, that much was clear. But even if we mortgaged the company and spent every cent on planes, amenities, and capital projects, without the engagement of our employees, it wouldn't move the needle on winning back customers.

A few hours later, as we approached Chicago, I looked out of the window and could see the Willis Tower directly below.

It's going to be a nice place to live, I thought once again.

When we finally were assigned a gate, we deplaned and I thanked Jenna and her colleagues, wanting to tell them the news and ask them what I should tackle first. But that would have to wait for another twelve hours or so.

If you fly through O'Hare regularly, then you may know that there is a particular intersection within F Terminal that is heavily used by United customers. As I approached this junction, I noticed that the sign for baggage claim was a bit confusing. It seemed to indicate that you could turn either left or right. In fact, only one direction got you there, and I am sure thousands of people had made the wrong turn because of that sign. "Huh," I noted to myself, "that's confusing. We'll have to change that."

If you travel through O'Hare today, that sign has been fixed. It would prove to be one of the easier changes to be made; things would get harder from here—a lot harder. I felt like I was looking up at Mount Everest, preparing to summit—and I hadn't even reached base camp yet.

The bags took forever to reach the carousel, and while I waited with my fellow passengers, I recalled a comment I had made to Henry when he made me the offer. "If I take this job," I told him, "I am going to throw my whole heart into it." Henry agreed.

In retrospect, I probably should've used a different expression.

CHAPTER 8

REVIVAL

As far as I knew, it was the same day as my heart attack when they finally brought me out of the coma and extubated me—removing the tube that reached down my windpipe. It had to be explained to me that seven days had elapsed and the world had changed—or at least mine had.

By this time, Brett had taken over as interim CEO. The family had become immediate experts in cardiovascular care. My eyesight was slowly recovering after days in darkness. My body was completely atrophied. I couldn't have gotten up and walked away, even if I could manage to disentangle myself from the machines and all the other tubes sticking into my body. At this point, I felt I was more machine than man, hooked up to various complicated devices that performed all my bodily functions for me—and I do mean everything.

Though I don't distinctly remember it, I am told that I asked if we could still make it to the USC–Notre Dame game and wasn't happy when I found out that the Irish had trounced our Trojans. Dr. Flaherty, a Notre Dame grad, was elated for his Irish and enjoyed kidding me about it.

It took several days before I was fully conscious and alert, as I transitioned from dreamless sleep to a different kind of nightmarish, twilight existence. An immense cocktail of drugs and other substances scorched through my system, bringing with them a million conflicting side effects as

I tried to regain my bearings. I can be candid now and say hallucinations—highly vivid—were among them, some of which produced a tad of concern, while others produced rip-roaring laughter, especially from my kids.

Late at night, I would often startle the nurses, claiming with utter seriousness that I saw either Brett or Kate standing in my hospital room. I would try to get up out of bed, not advisable since my muscles were too weak to support me. I would have weeks of physical therapy to look forward to, learning to walk again.

My dosage of four hydrocodone tablets a day kept the pain away, mostly, but also increased my already heightened sense of disorientation and fear. In my more lucid moments, I would ask my nurses what level of crazy I had been through the night. "Just the right level of crazy," they assured me, even commenting that I was so convincing at times that they nearly took me seriously when I told them I saw a Brett Hart–like apparition in the night. My impulse was to immediately call United's chairman of the board, Henry Meyer, to assure him that I was all right and would be back in the office ASAP.

Fortunately, the wiser heads belonging to my nurses, doctors, and family prevailed. Cathy's brother, John Moulton, was relaying developments to the board, they assured me.

On one of my first days of wakefulness, I almost jumped out of bed, and pointed at the TV, telling everyone, "Look, look. It's Brett!"

Everyone in the room rolled their eyes, but I wasn't hallucinating this time. Brett was on television, for real. Local news was covering his visit to O'Hare, where he was meeting with our Tech Ops teams, trying to quell a storm that had erupted out of our ongoing negotiations with their union representatives, the International Association of Machinists and Aerospace Workers (IAM).

My heart story had remained the subject of heated attention, especially in the local Chicago media market, as reporters tried to pry daylight between United—Brett, the board, and employees—and its stricken, hospital-bound CEO. TV cameras remained staked outside the hospital, but whether they were pursuing our story we couldn't know for sure.

I felt guilty that Brett was standing in for me, taking the heat in my place, which motivated me to get better.

• • •

Northwestern not only is a preeminent center for cardiac care but it also ranks among the best teaching hospitals in the nation.

At least once a day, a group of doctors in training, interns, residents, and fellows—looking impossibly young—would file into my room and the attending physician would quiz them on my diagnosis and course of treatment.

I came to dread these sessions. My nurses, who at this point had formed a protective shield around me, explained that if I didn't get out of bed and at least start to look like I was improving, the endless cycle of drugs and medical interventions would never cease. "You've got to get your ass out of bed, if just for a bit, Oscar," they said.

So I hatched a conspiracy with them to make me look like the model of a healthy patient.

When they saw a group of doctors or residents making their rounds in halls near my room, a few of the male nurses would lift my body, limp from the atrophy, into a chair and clean me up a bit. Though I had lost forty-five pounds during the coma, it still took three of them to execute the incredibly painful and awkward maneuver. When the doctors entered the room, they saw me propped upright, hair combed, looking like I was ready to be discharged. The moment they left, the nurses would lift me up again, put me back in the hospital bed, and give me another hydrocodone tablet to ease the pain.

As one day followed the next, I did gradually improve. I felt my strength and my personality restored to me, bit by bit. The question transitioned from one of mere survival to how I would start on the road to recovery.

At this point, Dr. Allen Anderson, head of Northwestern's Bluhm Cardiovascular Institute, had taken charge of my care. As gregarious and full-hearted as he is brilliant, Dr. Anderson has become a dear friend.

However, it must be said, that's not how things started out. In those initial days, his clinical matter-of-factness rarely left me or my family members feeling better after a conversation with him. He was not one to err on the side of optimism or tell us what we wanted to hear. He was blunt about my chances of pulling through, even at a significantly diminished level, either physically or cognitively. Even with all the miracles of modern science and the combined brainpower and technological resources of one of the finest medical centers on the planet, "sometimes," he told my family, "it comes down to the fighting spirit of the patient and the loved ones."

"You don't know our dad," our kids were fond of saying in reply. I am sure Dr. Anderson had heard such sentiments—defiant courage masking anxiety—many times before.

Shortly thereafter, a new member would join him on visits, Dr. Duc Thinh Pham.

Dr. Pham was soft-spoken, with a gentle bedside manner. His family left Vietnam after the war and came to America, where his talents allowed him to rise to the top of his profession, running the heart transplant program at Tufts in Boston. Only two months earlier he had moved to Chicago to become surgical director for the Center for Heart Failure at Northwestern Medicine.

Dr. Anderson informed me that they would need to surgically implant a left ventricular assist device (LVAD) because my heart was basically shot. An LVAD is either a bridge to a full recovery or a stopgap measure to buy time for a heart transplant, the doctors explained.

Still in denial about my condition, I argued with them—the drugs and disorientation making me ornerier than my true personality. "You're not implanting anything in me!" I protested, or something to that effect.

The LVAD wasn't optional—it was do or die. "But I will never have a heart transplant!" I said firmly. If I had known of Dr. Pham's reputation as a world-class heart transplant surgeon—and understood that's why he was there in the first place—I would have deduced that they had already determined the heart transplant was necessary.

The continued dosages of mood-altering painkillers and the endless interventions began to take their toll on me mentally. For example, my lungs were filling with fluids, and for that reason doctors had prescribed no hydration, except when they needed to give me some water to simply stay alive. I would plead for water and be denied, only to be inundated with it when I didn't want it.

"Can you just explain to me what the hell you're doing, exactly. I'll do whatever you say, I just need to know the reasons," I would often say to Dr. Anderson. After one four-letter-word-laden outburst, so out of character for me, my kids turned to Dr. Anderson and said, "Told you he had a fighting spirit."

He and I laugh about these fights now—our experiences together would be the basis for a lifelong friendship. My account remains in debit with so many who extended extraordinary kindnesses to me, without even pausing to wonder if I deserved it. That's especially true of my nurses and the hospital staff who cared for me, whom I came to revere. They reminded me of the frontline people at United, "the people who do the work and deliver it," to quote the book of wisdom according to Mama Josefina yet again.

They saw me at my most helpless. None of the nurses, at this point, knew I was the chief executive of a big company, nor would it have mattered anyway in the middle of the night as they worked to clean and bathe me—while I apologized ceaselessly for inconveniencing them. If you or a loved one have ever spent time in a hospital for long stretches, you know that the nights are the loneliest, and it's the nurses who become your guardian angels—spiritually as much as medically.

On one occasion, in either the long hours of the night or the small hours of the morning—I can't quite recall—one of my nurses started to chat with me as she changed my soiled linens, rolling me from one side to the other as she talked. A woman of Indian heritage in her middle forties, she told me something I've never forgotten.

"There are two kinds of patients in your condition," she explained as she carried on with her duties. "There are those who look at what just happened to them and ask, 'Why me?'—as in, 'Why did this misfortune befall me, rather than somebody else.'"

She continued, "And then, there are the patients who look at what they just survived, how lucky they are, and they ask, 'Why me?'—as in, 'Why was I spared? What's still in store for me? What is it that I should do with this gift?'"

I was determined to be the latter sort of person.

Often, as she explained to me, the difference depends on whether the patient feels a sense of purpose, motivated by the knowledge that people are counting on them and there remains some great work left for them to do in life.

If she was correct—and I know that she was—then the people of United were as responsible for my miraculous recovery as anyone. What they did next not only saved my job but also saved my life.

I was at my lowest point and in denial about the severity of my condition. I was even teetering on the verge of becoming that first sort of patient my nurse described, falling into a sense of victimhood.

That was when the mail started coming in, piles and piles of mail, almost all of it from United employees, some of it from folks I had met during the listening tour, many from those I hadn't. I could scarcely believe it. Day after day, messages poured in from around the world.

Hundreds, then thousands. Emails and text messages, social media posts, even prayer cards that promised rosaries were being said on my behalf.

Many of them were letters, packages sent to my home address, presents and goodies that my family shared with the hospital staff and patients up and down the ICU ward. Employees at airports around the world had created GET WELL OSCAR banners, and hundreds of them signed their names. Employees from as far as Guam, Micronesia, and Hawaii signed with their distinctive signatures of friendship. "Hafa Adai!" (pronounced *half-a-day*), across Guam and the Mariana Islands, is the friendly Chamorro greeting. Also, "Kaselehlie," or "Hello" in Pohnpeian, a Micronesian language. And, of course, from Hawaii, "Aloha, we will meet again."

When I awoke each morning, my kids would take turns reading me the letters. Nine a.m. was the sacrosanct hour known as "the daily reading," an inviolable bloc in our schedule where they would read every note to me.

They were full of well-wishes for me personally. But behind every kind word was a deeper, more urgent wish for us to continue what we had started in those first thirty-seven days. It seemed that word of my visits had gotten around, and people believed that I meant what I said.

I'd been granted so little time to spend with employees before my heart attack that I didn't dare let myself believe that I had even begun to forge a genuine connection with them, much less that my heart story would resonate with so many people.

With every letter the kids read to me, I wanted to repay back tenfold the kindnesses to each member of my United family—and do it personally.

Months later, while I recovered from my heart transplant surgery in the hospital, I got the chance of a lifetime to do precisely that. My transplant coordinator discreetly let me now that she had just evaluated a patient who had suffered heart failure and had been admitted to the cardiac care unit.

"His name is Fernando Falcone and he is a United flight attendant, Oscar. I was wondering if you wanted to—"

"Can I meet him?!" I jumped in.

She wheeled me over the airport-length distances of the hospital campus, and as we walked into Fernando's room, she said, "I'll make quick introductions and come back in a few minutes, okay?"

A smile on my face, I gently explained that given that both Fernando and I were Latino, I was willing to wager that we'd have more to talk about than just a few minutes would allow.

Boy, I was right. When the door to Fernando's ICU room opened and he saw me wheel in, wearing the same hospital gown as him, he burst into tears. Then his husband burst into tears, as did I. I looked behind me to the heart transplant coordinator, and she was in tears. We shared stories of our lives and families. We talked about United and I listened to him tell me about his experience.

Of all the cardiac wards in all the hospitals in all the world, I'd rolled into his. It was a strange coincidence.

But, quite quickly, we forgot all about our common employer; our common mortal challenge established a far deeper connection. Fernando would also require a heart transplant to survive, and I hoped my story would lift his spirits.

It was a meeting of hearts, one frail heart to another. In the years since my recovery, to this day, I still show up to the hospital, often during holidays or the night shift, when I know people are starving for company, and I tell them about Fernando.

The letters from United people had fortified my spirits when they were flagging. I was happy to have the opportunity to redirect all of that kindness and share it with him.

After weeks of feeling helpless and being consoled by others, I finally felt that I had retaken my sense of agency, simply by the act of providing strength to someone else—and a frontline employee to boot.

After a couple of hours of conversation, Fernando asked if we could take a picture and if he could post it on social media, and I said, "Of course." The image of the two of us, our smiles frozen in time, remains indelibly branded into my mind.

My nurse was right. I had important duties ahead of me—to be there with Cathy to watch our kids thrive, to enjoy the wonderful adults they'd become, and to cherish the families they themselves would one day raise.

And I had a meaningful project still ahead that people depended on me to see through, one that I had begun two months earlier.

CHAPTER 9

"COME ON, THERE'S ROOM FOR YOU!"

It's the kind of thing that happens in corporate or legal thrillers. First thing in the morning, on that Tuesday after Labor Day, in what would be my first day at United, each member of the executive team received calls instructing them to report directly to the offices of Craig Martin's law firm.

They arrived, one by one, and took seats around the conference table. The war room vibes had disappeared—the discarded fast-food wrappers and empty Dunkin Donuts coffee cups had been removed.

"They're here. This is it," Craig said, as he stuck his head in the office where Brett and I were nervously waiting. The three of us walked down the hallway and entered the room.

Craig had offered to deliver the news so I wouldn't be the one seen as wielding the knife, but I felt it was important that I assumed the responsibility.

I briefly explained the process that had led up to the decision for the company to part ways with the CEO, as well as with several other colleagues, and that I would be taking over effective immediately.

As they absorbed the news, I studied the faces of each person who now comprised my team—and three people in particular.

Gerry Laderman was acting chief financial officer, dubbed by Wall Street as the father of the aircraft purchasing deals; since he was the former longtime treasurer of Continental, the two of us went way back. Gerry was a descendant of Holocaust survivors, and his razor-sharp mind and financial acumen were softened by his kindly demeanor and generous spirit. He would modernize United's fleet and become a key player in our future growth strategy that, ultimately, proved to be the crowning achievement of our turnaround.

There was Greg Hart, head of operations—the same role that I had occupied at CSX. Operations would be the cornerstone, making Greg a pivotal figure. Until United started improving our on-time reliability, our turnaround wouldn't get off the ground. Our costs would continue to soar and our customer service would continue to plummet unless we started getting those planes in the air with greater reliability and reduced turnround time.

I happened to notice that Linda Jojo, chief information officer, was wearing a particularly tense expression. And I would soon find out why when we returned to the United offices.

"Look," I recall saying, "we've all known and worked with each other for a long time, given my long board tenure. I will be getting up to speed, and I will be relying on each of you to help me. I'll be touching base with you individually, but for now, let's all go back to work as usual."

There was no need for introductory remarks. We all knew one another too well for that, and it wasn't the moment for a grand speech. In any case, I wanted all of us back in the office by the time employees heard the news.

My goal was to change what it felt like to work at United, to empower people rather than dictate to them, and that was going to start with how we communicated this leadership change.

Employees would rightfully be concerned about what it would mean for the airline, for their colleagues, and for themselves. I wanted them to see that their senior leaders were in the office, present and ready to answer their questions—and to listen.

As the meeting broke up, I thanked Craig and Brett for all their hard work since February, and I also made a note to thank Henry, John Walker, and Dave Vitale. Somehow, they had managed a complex investigation, developed a succession plan, and implemented a delicate transition—all without leaks or public acrimony.

I felt sorry for the executives who had become caught up in this fiasco, including the outgoing CEO. I knew them as colleagues and friends, and I was anguished for what this might mean for their careers as well as for their families. But I also felt proud of our board for the way they'd conducted themselves. We had done it by the book.

Megan told me there was an SUV downstairs that was waiting to take me to our offices at the Willis Tower. I preferred to walk, I said—it was only a few blocks, and the weather was wonderful. Megan insisted that I take the car, my first introduction to the new realities of CEO-hood. I complied.

I hadn't become comfortable with the idea of niceties like a private car; it didn't feel "like me." But once I started chatting with Margaret, the driver, I quickly discovered that she had an extraordinary story. She had immigrated from Poland and invested her life savings in the car I was riding in. It was her own "business on wheels," her life's work. Predawn drives to O'Hare, late-night pickups after dinners with corporate customers—over the next few years, Margaret's vehicle would become my mobile office and she was a trusted ear to talk with. Thanks, Margaret, and drive safely, my friend.

• • •

As we crossed the river and approached the Willis Tower, my phone buzzed. Our press release and my letter to employees had just gone out into the world. The die was cast—no turning back now.

Margaret took us down the ramp that leads to Lower Wacker Drive—the bottom layer of the double-decker roadway that encircles Chicago's Financial District's skyscrapers and grants access to the basement loading docks. "Sonja's waiting for you there," Margaret explained.

"Hey, Margaret," I said, "do you mind if we just pull up to the main entrance? I'd prefer to just walk in through the lobby like everyone else."

A few moments later, we pulled up in front of the building. I wasn't a very well-known face at the company—not yet anyway—so I slipped anonymously into the crowd of employees streaming through the revolving doors into the airy two-story-tall atrium lobby.

Sonja joined up with me and the two of us filed through the security gates and shuffled behind a group of waiting employees who were trying to get into an open elevator. "We'll wait for the next one," I told the group as they held the doors open. "No, no, come on, there's room for you," they insisted, waving us in.

We tried to make ourselves as skinny as possible, squeezing between employees as they sipped their Starbucks coffees and checked morning emails on their phones. As we rode up, I could tell that people around me were just now reading the news, sharing their surprise with one another. I noticed a few people dart their eyes at me as they matched the picture on their phone with my face.

I gave a sheepish grin. "Good morning, everyone."

The doors opened on the eleventh floor, our stop, and I waved to the group as I exited. "Have a great day, folks. I'll be seeing all of you soon."

We entered the foyer of United's C-Suite—a place I knew well from my years on the board, but this time the atmosphere felt different, more charged. Young staffers moved briskly through the corridors, almost pressing themselves up against the wall when I passed—as if we were a crew in a submarine. I stopped and made sure to ask the names of everyone, even as Sonja hurried me on the way to my new office.

It was absurdly large scaled, wrapping around the corner of the building, with nearly as much square footage as my temporary apartment unit. The previous CEO's things had been removed, making the place feel even more cavernous.

"We could fit at least another office in here," I told Sonja. Eventually, we cut the space in half, creating an office right next to mine. It would become Kate Gebo's when I hired her as chief of staff two weeks later.

I noticed that the televisions in the office were showing coverage about United. I assumed the financial networks were reporting on the transition. Instead, they were going live with a story about a massive IT problem at United Airlines that was causing cascading delays across our operations. It was yet another problem stemming from the failure to merge the systems of Continental and United.

A few minutes later, as I was walking the floor, saying hello to folks, I spun around and accidentally ran headfirst into Linda Jojo as she raced to her office in full crisis mode. Now I understood why she seemed especially tense during the meeting at Craig's office earlier in the morning.

Her expression made clear what she was thinking: "This can't be happening on the new boss's first day!"

By the end of the day her team ably solved the problem, but it provided a useful reminder that the airline doesn't stop for a day because there's a new person in charge. The IT issue demonstrated, yet again, just how much farther we had to go toward true integration.

It also illustrated the costliness of disunity at every level of the organization—between the legacy employee groups; between headquarters and the front line; between divisions within headquarters itself—something I noticed immediately as I began touring the building, introducing myself to employees.

I started with the highest floors that United occupied and worked my way down—beginning with the Network Operations Center, the heart and brains of United's global operation.

At each floor, I didn't give advance warning and it was always amusing to see faces pop up above the parapets of their cubicles, trying to see what the commotion was about, evidently surprised to see the CEO casually strolling through the upper or lower reaches of the building.

The welcome was warm but cautious. Unlike frontline employees with union backing, these were corporate "at-will" employees, and I could tell they were cautious with their words, perhaps concerned to be overheard speaking too frankly about what changes needed to be made.

By contrast, when breaking news of the shake-up at the top of United began flashing on the television monitors in airport terminals across the country, I'm told it was met by rounds of cheers from both employees and customers. Spontaneous celebrations broke out in employee break rooms from Newark Liberty to LAX, O'Hare to Houston, with the kind of hugging and dancing reminiscent of a liberated populace. The approval was not of me, of course—most people had no idea who I was. Rather, they welcomed the prospect of much-needed change—any kind of change.

For once, United's passengers and the workforce that served them were united by a shared sentiment. Alas, it was their common disdain for the service that had beleaguered them both. And, also, more optimistically, they were united by a hope that whatever came next might prove better than what they'd known for so long.

I returned to my bare, cavernous office and checked my emails. Megan's communications team had already compiled clips of the news coverage. I opened a link to CNBC's *Squawk on the Street.*

"United/Continental shares under a little pressure this morning," reported the anchor. "A little bit," chuckled Phil LeBeau, the news outlet's expert on all things airlines.

"Oscar Munoz is the new CEO at United. And he's got some challenges in front of him," Phil explained. "First and foremost, underperforming operations in a number of areas." He was right on that count. Against our biggest competitors, Delta and American Airlines, United consistently fell behind in profitability and reliability.

"There are unhappy pilots, and the flight attendants are still looking for a contract." He was right again. Relationships between the airline and labor were at an all-time low after more than a decade of bankruptcies leading to furloughs.

From the perspective of United's unions, it seemed like any time fuel spiked or demand dropped, the books got balanced on the backs of our employees, starting with the frontline workers, whose morale we rely on most and whose trust we can least afford to lose. Contract negotiations had dragged on for years, building up bad feelings, mounting up bad faith, and bringing down the quality of our service to customers and one another.

"And you've got a battered corporate image," he concluded.

"The bottom line is this," Phil said. "Oscar Munoz says the right things. But can he actually deliver that for United? Can it become a better airline and a better investment?"

That was the question on everyone's mind, including my own. My instinct told me the answer couldn't be glimpsed from behind my desk in the C-Suite. I needed to get out into the field and speak with employees and customers.

I knew I was living on borrowed time, and I would soon need to arrive at a solution that I could present to my team, the board, and investors, although I had no idea how limited my time really was.

With the blood clot growing in my heart, unbeknownst to me, I embarked on my listening tour, traveling to airports across the United network. Though it would be cut short thirty-seven days later, the tour would not fail to yield insights that led directly to United's turnaround.

CHAPTER 10

THE LISTENING TOUR

My first week on the job, I knew we needed to think differently about how United communicated—that is, if our turnaround strategy was to gain credence with a skeptical flying public and employee base. I picked up my phone and cold-called a few PR consultancy firms I knew by their reputations, including the eponymously named firm that was run by Richard Edelman, who would become a good friend.

Once I had convinced the firm's receptionist that, indeed, I really was who I said I was, she sent me to the voice mail box of Kevin Cook, managing director of public affairs for Edelman's Chicago office.

Kevin called back quickly, and the two of us discussed how we could begin to change the way the world felt about working for and flying with United. I liked the approach and told him to develop a strategy.

By the following Monday, his team had built an impressive communications road map for the next ninety days, which included the development of "United Airtime"—our digital platform to receive and analyze employee and customer feedback.

Next, the plan called for a charm offensive aimed at the traditional media as well as trade publications and blogs. They had cataloged United's woes for years and we would need to convince them that we were worth giving a second chance.

As a first step, I visited the offices of our local paper, the *Chicago Tribune*, and sat down for a lengthy back-and-forth with the editorial board. Next, we hosted a reporter from the *Wall Street Journal*, followed by half a dozen more interviews.

I told them about my first flight as CEO from Jacksonville to Chicago, and about my growing to-do list that I was accumulating—"The Top Ten Dumbest Things."

I had already begun ticking off a few items on my own list, beginning with formally renaming our headquarters to become the corporate support center (CSC) because that's what it is supposed to do: support the rest of the corporation, not the other way around—a small change, perhaps, but words matter, and such changes speak volumes across a global, diverse workforce like United's.

I was also dismayed to learn that the most senior members of the company didn't have a standing weekly meeting to discuss business results and metrics, progress on key strategic initiatives, and, importantly, coordinate their efforts toward a common aim.

With the help of Kate Gebo, we reorganized the structure and established weekly executive team meetings—the "E-Team." Every Monday, the executive vice presidents, and others whose input would be additive, gathered around the table and we went through ongoing projects. Some of the leaders were perplexed by this new process; a few felt that it infringed on their territory or cramped their style to explain how they ran their departments to others. I'm sure most of them felt that it would simply be a waste of valuable time.

This skepticism was quickly dispelled the first time that one member explained his or her priorities, which then instantly raised red flags with the others in the room. Redundancies that could have cost millions were quickly quashed before they arose. Conflicts that could have festered into large-scale problems were resolved preemptively. Communication and collaboration increased, and so did collegiality.

It's amazing what can happen when people start working together, when the left hand and the right know what each is doing, as I explained to journalists during my series of interviews.

I also told journalists about my conversations with frontline employees, of Jenna and Amy.

I had only just returned from my trip to our hub in Denver, where I met Amy. During that trip, I also visited one of our pilot training facilities. We were hoping to consolidate that location with a similar one in Houston; relocating the flight simulator facilities was a matter of great importance, but eliminating redundancies carried with it a political subtext, as it rankled the former Continental people. Located near the old Stapleton International Airport, the former main airport for the Mile High City, this was the home of a mock-up Boeing 737, where flight attendants could train and simulate real-world situations.

As they practiced giving their preflight safety briefings, drilled on how to prep for an emergency situation, and tested the inflatable rafts and slides for use during a water landing, I started chatting with the flight attendants as they took a break, in the fake cabin. I asked them all about what they wanted me to focus on first, and while many topics came up, one comment became canon: "Coffee and contracts, Oscar," that's what one flight attendant told me. She was right.

You'd never believe how far a good cup of coffee will go toward earning goodwill. During my walks through the Willis headquarters building in Chicago, employees explained to me that in a zeal to cut costs, no matter how small, all compostable coffee cups in employee break rooms were removed. Were there greater tragedies in the world? Of course. But I often think back to my tussles with Dr. Anderson, when I would tell him, "I'll follow doctors' orders, but I need to understand the reasons why you're doing what you're doing." There were no good answers behind these penny-pinching ideas—everyone knew that—and it sent a signal of disrespect.

It wasn't just employees getting the short end of the stick. On board our aircraft, we had severed our relationship with Starbucks and switched to a cheaper brand of coffee. It may seem like a small, insignificant decision, but it was the "stirring straw" that broke the camel's back—or at least it seemed to. It sparked a rebellion among frontline employees, especially veterans who remembered with fondness the days of high-quality offerings.

"I simply won't serve it," said one flight attendant to a member of my team. I'm not a coffee drinker and so I wouldn't know good coffee from bad, but the whole episode did leave a bitter taste in my mouth. Why should customers remain loyal to United when our product resembles that of a budget carrier's? Why should employees take pride in serving a substandard product at all? At best, the downgrades sent a mixed signal: "Care for the customer in the field," we seemed to be telling employees, "then watch as we cut back on the resources necessary for you to do it."

In the end, the savings from these efficiency drives were measly, which only proved how cheaply the company had been prepared to trade brand reputation and employee morale simply to buy a little bit of applause from Wall Street.

By the end of the year, we would make a significant investment in our coffee on board, partnering with the premium Italian roaster illy.

We would also go on to reverse another decision that had infuriated employees. One of the greatest aspects of working for an airline is the ability to fly on standby, and it's an especially attractive perk for United because we have the strongest global routes of any US airline. Like their colleagues at other carriers, our US-based employees had come to depend on these "Pass Travel" vouchers to stay connected to parents, spouses, and loved ones, especially if they live abroad.

A couple of employees had broken the rules by selling passes to others, which provided UA's leadership with an excuse to crack down, placing onerous restrictions on the program that, practically, rescinded the benefit. It was a classic case of a few bad apples, and there was no need to affect tens of thousands of employees in such a cruel and heartless manner just to send a message. We quickly reversed that policy and restored the employee pass travel system to the way it had always been.

Some of these changes happened within weeks of my arrival; others would take months to implement. And even if many of these improvements amounted to "small ball" in comparison to United's larger problems, they signaled that I was listening. They bought me some goodwill and, most important, time.

Next, in newspapers across the globe, we took out a full-page advertisement where we posted an open letter, which read, in part:

> To our passengers, my fellow employees and the communities where we live and work,
>
> Simply put, we haven't lived up to your expectations. That's going to change.
>
> My singular mission is to engage our passengers and employees every step of the way. I want to hear and implement your good ideas. I promise to show that we're listening and report on our progress.

Those were some bold promises, to be sure. As ever, I knew I would be held to them, and I wanted to live up to my mantra, "Proof, not promise." I needed to back up those words by personally showing up and putting in face time in our biggest business markets.

Of course, there were those for whom no gesture, however large, would be enough.

"I'm all for humble CEOs who don't profess to know everything," wrote an influential travel reporter. "In fact, he's about to embark on a 90-day learning tour. Yet that begs the obvious question: When the hell is United going to hire a boss who knows anything about running an airline?"

We were about to find out how much more I needed to learn.

• • •

Newark (EWR) was the next logical place to test run my turnaround message to our employees, as well as to the editorial board of the *New York Times*. We had some work to do in repairing the self-inflicted damage we'd done to our brand in the tristate area. On October 1, 2015, two weeks before my heart attack, we touched down on the tarmac of Newark

Liberty International Airport, which serves the crucial New Jersey–New York area.

A few years prior, United had signaled a partial retreat from this market, selling our coveted landing slots at JFK International Airport to Delta. That decision was United's loss but a big win for our rivals Delta and JetBlue, granting them a free lane to build their New York franchises. It was emblematic of the "shrink to growth" strategy that defined United in years past. I was determined not to repeat those mistakes. I wanted to signal that United was ready to reverse the complacency that had set us behind in New York–New Jersey and that we were ready to start winning back business everywhere we flew.

As I walked off the airplane and into the gate area, Megan trailing behind me, we were met by a wall of United employees who burst into a deafening roar of whoops of celebration and applause, clapping, and jumping up and down. I looked behind me to see if there was a world-famous celebrity walking off the jet bridge behind me. "Was Jagger on the flight or something?" I laughed.

Even as I recount it years later, I feel the same sense of unworthiness for what my employees were expressing, matched by a resolve to not let them down. As they surrounded us, their arms outstretched for hugs and high fives, taking group selfies, customers began gathering around as well to find out what was going on. It's not every day that you see airline employees break out into spontaneous acts of celebration, and it had been a long time since there had been much to celebrate at United.

Perhaps they weren't as "disenchanted, disenfranchised and disengaged" as I'd feared and suggested during my interviews.

But when employees pulled me in closer for a hug, they would often make a comment, an aside, nothing major but unforgettable, that let me know that things were definitely not okay.

"Not waving but drowning" is how I would come to think of these celebratory scenes; they were really cries for someone to recognize that the people of United needed help, fast.

A key purpose of the visit was to have lunch with the leaders who managed the hub at EWR, a chance for a meet and greet and to learn about the operation. Newark Liberty was once the location of one of our largest kitchens, where hundreds of UA employees prepared the food served in every travel class as well as in the United lounges—we call it the catering operations.

"Instead of having lunch at some restaurant," the EWR team suggested, "why don't we have lunch at our own catering facility?" It would be a great opportunity for me to tour the kitchen facilities and meet with some employees who rarely get paid a visit by senior leaders.

Each catering shift is staffed by a few hundred workers. I didn't know this in advance, but in preparation to greet us, the EWR team had subdivided the employees into smaller groups so I could meet with each, one at a time. And each group was given placards with a letter of my name— O-S-C-A-R.

When I walked into the kitchen that day, it was bedlam. The attempt for the groups to be subdivided was quickly abandoned as the workers, predominately Hispanic and largely female, rushed toward us—singing, clapping, chanting songs. As I hugged and thanked everyone—shouting to be heard—I automatically reverted to speaking Spanish—or as close to it as I could muster.

As I looked into the eyes of each person who wanted to shake my hand or get a high five, I saw the soft features and kind eyes reminiscent of my grandmother Mama Josefina. These employees knew hard work, as she did. But had any of them experienced the type of generosity that my grandmother had received on that day when her bosses in hotel management bid her a touching retirement farewell? I doubted it, and that was the point. This was perhaps the first time they had ever witnessed a CEO deigning to walk into the kitchens. I knew for certain it was the first time they had met a CEO who looked like them and spoke the language the way they did.

This was a first for me, too. I had spent much of my career hiding my heritage, something I will discuss in later chapters. Now I realized the hidden strengths that my background and life experience might provide in connecting with employees.

The enthusiasm was genuine—no doubt about that. But I knew better than to think that the underlying problems at United had been solved simply thanks to a change in leadership. Far from it. The outpouring of goodwill was an expression of hope but not necessarily of trust. It could turn quickly if I failed to deliver proof to back up my promises.

We exited the kitchen, and I sat down in an adjoining conference room for lunch, joined by the senior leaders who run the Newark hub. I asked them how things were going (my deep questions, once again). They were cagey at first but eventually began to open up and I started to hear the words "Project Quality" quite a lot. They were referring to a new working group back at headquarters; it was the taskmaster appointed to manage the cost-savings drive.

On a recent earnings call, the company had promised investors that the airline would realize $1 billion in savings over time. As a result, everyone was having to do more with less—certainly for efficiency, but it also felt to the field officers like it was mostly to make good on promises made to investors.

They were having an issue with the baggage handling operations, otherwise known as the ramp (the team you see below the wing, loading your luggage when you've boarded). "Well, let's go down there and talk to them," I said.

In the break room for ramp employees, I could tell they were not prepared for the CEO and our team, which was exactly what I wanted. It took a few attempts at opening them up, but once they felt free to express themselves, there was no holding back.

"Well, what the hell do you expect, Oscar!" was the sum of the response. "You've cut dozens of people from our shift."

This was Project Quality, striking again.

"Okay," I said. "I actually know the guy at the head of Project Quality who is in charge of making these cuts, and in fact he used to run EWR. Why don't I bring him to you so he can present his facts and logic about these cuts with all of you. You may not agree entirely, but at least you'll know why the cuts have been made," I added.

I am always willing to listen to complaints. Sometimes they're fact-based, sometimes not. In this case, the frontline employees were absolutely right. The cost-saving drives meant to hit the $1 billion target had resulted in cuts to staffing that simply didn't make sense and were bound to hurt our operational reliability and annoy our customers. Based on that, we reversed course and rehired many of the affected employees.

As much as I appreciated the enthusiastic response from some employees, what I really valued were these hard truths. And I was just getting started.

The next stops on my tour would remind me how far I had to go in rebuilding trust.

A few days later, I landed in Houston, home of the old Continental headquarters, where many employees still resented that United's hometown of Chicago had become the combined global headquarters.

In the middle of the night, when planes take a brief break from flying, United Tech Operations, maintenance, and repair teams go to work.

After treating a select group of frontline employees to a private dinner in the city, we returned to the airport. And sometime around midnight, I was ushered past a parking lot packed with pickup trucks and into a crowded break room. I was handed a microphone that snapped, crackled, and popped like a radio transmission from Mars. Before me were the angry faces of a few hundred workers—rough-hewn, mostly bearded, each bearing a map of the world written on their faces, as the expression goes. The temperature ran hot because their resentments ran deep.

Since this was the start of the main shift, as planes only stop at night, this group was fresh and rested. I, on the other hand, was on hour fifteen of a workday that spanned multiple time zones, and the day wasn't over yet, not by a long shot. The intense humidity of late summer in Houston, in the unair-conditioned hangar, and in the dead of night, left me drenched in sweat.

I admit, I didn't exactly fit in—at least at first. All of them were geared up in their high-vis jackets, knee pads, and protective equipment, while I was wearing my white collared shirt and rolled-up shirtsleeves. I tried to break the ice but, given the expanse of the room and the large crowd, I couldn't quite gain a captive audience. I felt a little bit like the president of the fraternity in the film classic *Animal House*, trying and failing to bring a rowdy group to order so they could hear me earnestly talk about my plans to turn things around.

For the Houston Tech Ops team on shift that evening, they probably felt it was more akin to the movie *Groundhog Day*: same shit, different day, and yet another CEO promising to "make things better."

They didn't know me or what I stood for. Only a few days had passed since many of them first heard my name. Most of them probably assumed I was another yet "suit," standing in front of them making a new set of flimsy promises.

This is a room where titles take a back seat to experience, and I hadn't earned the right to lecture to people who had been on the job long before I arrived and would likely be there long after my stint ended (however long that proved to be).

I had earned the respect of many large groups of employees in my past jobs, but that didn't matter here. I had spent much of my time as chief operating officer at CSX walking around the yards and facilities of that network, interacting with union employees, many of whom have very long tenures with the company. Now, I was starting from scratch with a new cohort of union maintenance workers who had made no secret of their disdain and general foul mood toward United management.

It didn't take a moment to realize that my cheerful greeting was being drowned out by sneers and catcalls that made the faulty microphone obsolete.

"You suck."

"Get out of here."

"I've heard that bullshit before."

Instinct told me to drop the mic and get to the middle of the room, so I hopped onto the picnic table and then onto the next and the next until I was surrounded by my audience. One rancorous voice had been louder than all the others and so I kept leaping until I found myself before an enormous man who seemed to hold sway over his peers.

Sometimes it's more important to get a few people's attention than it is to hold everyone at rapt focus. I stood in front of him, raised my voice so everyone could hear me, and introduced myself to him.

"I'm here trying to listen but you're yelling and telling me to fire people and do things that simply are not actionable," I told him.

"Yeah, well, we've heard it all before," he said angrily.

I hopped down from the table so as not to be talking down to him. But he was a big guy and now he loomed way above me—and I'm not especially short, either. With all eyes fixed on the two of us, I couldn't back down. I could see out of my peripheral vision that our Houston Tech Ops station manager, Rodney Lutzen, was getting slightly nervous. Would he have to intervene?

It wouldn't be the best headline if the new United CEO was knocked out in a brawl.

"You're telling me the CEO of this airline has stood in front of all of you, in the middle of the night, not just talking but really asking for your opinion on what's needed?"

Everyone knew the answer was "No."

Granting little and giving no ground, we were both pretty emotional at this point, but for different reasons. He looked like he wanted to deck me, and I would not have been surprised if he tried. Coming from CSX railroad, I was accustomed to facing rough-and-tumble union workers. It helped that I'd grown up around and was raised by men and women who knew hard work.

I knew that like my dad, a blue-collar immigrant and lifelong union member, he had a family to feed and was looking out for them. With every eye and ear glued to our conversation, the crowd took a break and began to listen, and I began to hear their concerns and their hopes.

I've learned—often through failures—that saying you're committed to listening and actually doing so are two different things. Active listening takes patience and perseverance when, regardless of status, your colleagues are on your ass. Having the fortitude to listen is hard but essential.

Like opening an emergency release valve, the pressure began to come down and more people felt that they could get into the conversation.

"Look," I said. "All I am asking is that you listen to what I have to say, tell me what I need to hear, but you have to do it in a way that I can put it into action." I wouldn't promise what I couldn't deliver, and I wouldn't necessarily agree with their criticisms unless the facts supported it. But I understood that employees' perceptions were reality. Even if they were inaccurate about certain facts, or if I didn't agree with them, their anger and frustration were real, and therefore I took them seriously.

After much intense back-and-forth, I hadn't won him over, or anyone else for that matter, but that wasn't what was most important. I knew I had made an impression. He and the other guys probably still thought I was full of shit, and how could I blame them?

To them, I must've come across just like every new CEO who dons a hard hat, shakes some hands, and is never heard from again—not until, that is, he exits the company with a golden parachute, leaving a mess behind. I had to prove to them that this time would be different, that I was different.

The following morning, by the time I landed at our next stop in Los Angeles, my hometown, word had gotten around about my exchange with the group in Houston. The second I left Houston, they must've gotten on their phones and started texting one another about it.

On the flight, I started reading employee and industry-wide message boards and saw, to my delight, some genuine surprise among people that I was serious about visiting with everyone. But most of the comments were "I'll believe it when I see it."

At LAX, I made my way to a break room located just off the tarmac and ramp area—the "below the wing" area of our operations. I wasn't shocked to find the same pissed-off expression as their colleagues in Houston. Then I noticed something that most corporate leaders probably are trained to ignore because it's not politically correct.

"Jeez," I thought to myself, "a lot of these guys are Latino."

They reminded me of people I had grown up with. In fact, it wouldn't have surprised me if many of them lived near the same neighborhood where I had grown up.

I had to be realistic. I knew I wasn't going to win these guys over by wasting their lunch break and telling them about my problems. Just introducing myself and building some kind of rapport would be a win. It also felt good just to be back home in L.A., among a group of people who reminded me of my old friends and neighbors. I took a chance.

"Orale!" I shouted—Mexican street slang roughly meaning "Yo, what's up?" but a universally known term in that area regardless of your ethnicity. I knew for damn sure that no other CEO had ever uttered that phrase in front of them.

The ice I'd felt just evaporated, and those passive faces broke into wide smiles. I didn't have to talk about United; we just talked about our community, our heritage, and our opportunity. I saw over the tops of hard hats that the crowd in the back was getting bigger and people were straining to hear, so I started taking questions for as long as people were willing to talk. Afterward a manager came up to tell me that it was the first time he'd ever heard from an employee, of Latino heritage, who had kept to himself for years but eagerly participated in the back-and-forth discussion with me.

Perhaps it wasn't as important that I proved to employees that I had all the answers to every problem. If I simply I demonstrated that, before I intended to lead, I wanted to listen and learn from them, perhaps that would be enough to generate goodwill.

Sure, a lot of the comments from these employees were about nuts-and-bolts issues that mattered to their paychecks, pensions, and quality of work life; there were many things that were broken and needed fixing. But if I could just break down this wall of distrust, it would be more important than getting every tactical decision right. The only way to do that was to speak honestly about where I came from, how I was raised, and the values my experiences in life had instilled in me.

I became convinced that the task at hand would be one of rekindling that love for what we do. The rest, I was sure, would follow.

The final leg of the tour took me to our hub at San Francisco on a beautiful Sunday afternoon. United was hosting its annual Family Day, an employee appreciation event that coincides with the Bay Area's Air and Water Show.

As the renowned and award-winning United barbecue team served up their sizzling fare, we mingled on the tarmac outside the hangars; parents enjoyed the company of their peers, while children watched in awe as airplanes of every vintage and brand zipped overhead in tight formation.

I spent the day on the vast grounds that make up United's maintenance and repair facilities, talking with families and vendors. As employees sang the national anthem and the airplanes danced across the sky, the extraordinary skill of these stunt aviators reminded me of the remarkable industry I was privileged to work in. I hoped the impressive display also inspired the young people who were there, perhaps allowing them to imagine the day when they might take to the skies themselves, "slipping the surly bonds of earth," making aviation their life's calling.

It was fun, exhausting, and so, so very rewarding.

• • •

And now, we return to that fateful morning of my heart attack.

After two weeks on the road, the following day I returned to Chicago. The next morning, while running along the Chicago lakefront—not knowing that a heart attack was but an hour away—I found myself contemplating the past few weeks.

After my final sprint, I took it easy and jogged the rest of the way back to my apartment. My breath was visible in the mid-October air, but it wasn't cold. I looked east at the dawn of a new day. The sun's rays heated the moisture vapor that rose from Lake Michigan, creating a dayglow haze in the atmosphere—it was as though the horizon disappeared so the sky and the waters could meet.

I thought about the people I met in the EWR kitchens, in the hangars at Houston, L.A., and San Francisco. And I thought how much they reminded me of the people I grew up with and who raised me. Above all, I thought about my late mother, Francisca.

She had tragically passed away before she could see me and my siblings truly succeed in life. She gave birth to me at such a young age, and so unexpectedly, when she was living in Mexico. The sacrifices she made so my brothers and sisters and I could make it to America I still cannot fathom. Could she ever have imagined what lay in store for me when I got here?

She surely would've been amazed at where our journeys led us, as I am amazed to see what heights my brothers and sisters, as well as their children, have climbed.

However, I don't believe that she would've been surprised to know that the values, culture, and language she instilled in me had become my most important asset. And she would've been satisfied to see me put them at the service of hardworking people who were very much like her.

Past and present had met, strangely, in my mind. I look back on the moment, just before I nearly lost my life, and contemplate how I got there in the first place.

CHAPTER 11

TIERRA CALIENTE

My story is a quintessentially American one, though it began in Mexico. My earliest years until about the age of eight were spent in places like Ciudad Juárez, where I was born, Chihuahua, Apatzingán, and the villages that dot the roads between them. I can still remember the first time I saw an airplane, which in the early 1960s was an exceedingly rare sight in the arid skies above the vast expanses of what is known as Tierra Caliente—literally, "Hot Land" in my native Spanish.

The road that cuts through the low-lying region of Michoacán state in west-central Mexico was the only way folks like my grandmother Mama Josefina and I could journey the roughly fifteen hundred miles between Juárez and Apatzingán in the summer of 1964. It's a charming little *pueblo* that, while beautiful, was mostly significant as the birthplace of Mexican independence.

It's taken my entire life to fit together the puzzle pieces of my family story, and even now I am discovering new twists and turns.

The story goes like this, and it begins in Juárez, a town that shares a border with the United States, opposite El Paso, Texas. At the tender age of twenty-three, my mother found out she was pregnant with a baby boy, me. Scared and confused, and with only her mother, Mama Josefina, to help her, my mom placed her hopes in her older brother, Humberto—Tio Beto—who had immigrated to the United States years earlier and had already risen to become a prominent leader in the California Mexican American labor movement. She had heard romantic stories of how he was fighting for justice, side by side in "la causa" with Cesar Chavez. Unfortunately, Tio Beto could obtain only a single visa for my mother on a limited work basis.

Uncertain of what to do but dreaming of giving me a better life in America, Mom reluctantly left me in the care of Mama Josefina and a friend, Elizabeth, so she could find work in "el Norte." That decision was the hardest in her life, but my mother knew the money to be earned by working in the States was so much greater if she went with her brother, Beto, to Los Angeles, with the plan that I would soon follow. But when that would be, we didn't know.

And that's how Mama Josefina and I came to travel the road to Apatzingán. The bus service could make the journey in a couple of days, but since Mama Josefina couldn't afford the price of tickets for both of us, our journey was often on foot.

Our living arrangement in Apatzingán also proved short-lived, but I still keep an old report card from the local elementary school as a clue and proof of my time there. (I did well in class, even back then.) We then stayed for a time with another of Mom's brothers, in Chihuahua City, until, eventually, a woman who was godmother to my mom invited us to live with her in Juárez. And so we pulled up stakes once more and headed back north.

I didn't realize it at the time, but as I look back, I now understand that the path that led me to where I ended up in life, my earliest preparations as a leader, began on those country roads throughout Mexico, roads that ultimately led me to the United States and to a destiny beyond my dreams.

"I am part of all I have met," so goes the poem "Ulysses." When I look at my life and the person I've become, I see the sum of many people who shaped my character and perspective, who helped me locate my north star and sent me on my entirely unlikely path through life, often keeping me on course when I lost my direction. The philosophy that I would apply, many decades later, to rallying the employees of CSX, and later at United, had its origins in the people and places I met along the way, starting with Mama Josefina.

An entirely uneducated woman, she would become my first and most enduring tutor in a simple but profound lesson: to lead is to serve. Indeed, though I was following *her* around the country, she was really serving me, even as she led me. I knew that she would put her body in front of harm's way to protect me, if necessary—fists first.

Never a woman of means, she taught me the meaning of the phrases "richness of spirit" and "the dignity of work." Her work ethic and stubborn optimism made it possible for me to make it to this country. Those values—her values—also ensured that I could "make it" in America once here. She had taught me to respect everyone; to truly empathize with the people around me.

My uncle also left an indelible impression on me from the moment I first met him in 1968, a year remembered as one of upheaval for the whole world and a year of uprooting for my little world.

He showed up in Juárez and told Mama Josefina and me to pack our things, which didn't take long. We were going to America, to Los Angeles. I didn't really appreciate the immensity of what that meant. For me, it was another town, another long road trip ahead.

When we finally arrived in Los Angeles, we were greeted by Tio's saintly wife, Margie, who welcomed Mama Josefina and me into their house, which sat on Fedora Street in what is now Koreatown. Just a few blocks away stood the campus of the University of Southern California, which I would eventually attend, making me the first in my entire family to go to college.

I remember his three daughters gathered around me like I was a newly found stray puppy. Thankfully, there was also Butchie, his son, who was near my age. He became my best friend while my three female cousins became my English tutors. I began picking it up quickly if only to get them to stop teasing me for being unable to speak a word of the language. This eclectic living arrangement didn't strike me as odd; it was just another new house with new people. Mama Josefina and I would do what we had always done and just learn to get along.

After a few weeks or months, I don't exactly recall, a group of people arrived at the house, and I could tell something big was happening. From a station wagon, for those who remember that vehicle type, out stepped a man whom Tio introduced as Eduardo Muñoz, with his family in tow. I had no idea that morning that the woman Eduardo called his wife was actually my mother; she had left when I was so young that I could not remember her.

When it was explained to me that, in fact, she was my true mother, and not Mama Josefina, my world seemed turned upside down. Yet, as most sons can attest, there was no confusion in her warm motherly embrace. I instantly understood that, after all our travels, I was finally home where I belonged.

Eduardo, her husband, was a different story. I was not yet ten, but I could instinctively tell that Eduardo didn't have the same affection for me as my mom did. I didn't understand then why he was so often very hard on me. It would take many years for this man who resented raising a boy who wasn't his own to finally—truly—become my father.

I arrived for my first day of American elementary school unable to speak a word of English. I didn't have much in the way of personal information records when I enrolled. The teacher took one look at my name on the student roster, Oscar Javier Camacho de Guzman, and decided for me that it needed shortening. She quickly scratched out everything but the Oscar and then asked me what my father's last name was. There was only Eduardo and so I replied, "Muñoz." That was my name from then on.

When she wrote the name, she forgot to add the tilde, which is that distinctive "Spanish mustache" that hangs over the *n* in Muñoz. Just like immigrants to Ellis Island, whose names were Americanized, the spelling stuck. I became a Munoz, not a Muñoz.

I anticipate that many friends and colleagues will have had little to no idea about this early chapter in my life, my childhood in Mexico, and my journey to America. They will likely be surprised to learn of it for the first time in this book, I imagine. It may seem strange to most people that I would want to keep such an integral part of my identity quiet for so long; even more surprising, perhaps, that it could be possible to do so in this age of social media and the internet, with all the digital bread crumbs we leave behind.

For most immigrants, however, especially those hailing from the southern hemisphere, such sentiments will ring a painfully familiar bell. Transplants of my generation closely guarded our family origin stories. Assimilation in those days often meant the annihilation of our cultural identity and leaving our heritage at the door when we walked into work each morning. Some immigrants choose to completely anglicize their names, with Pedros becoming Pauls, Marias becoming Marys, at least when at the office.

Of course, there's not much you can do with Oscar. In my new home of L.A., in Hollywood, Oscar is a coveted name—"The Oscar goes to . . ." I couldn't really have shortened or changed it up, even if I had wanted to. And I never did want to. I often say—to the eye-rolling of my millennial children—that I was a Dreamer long before DACA, long before anyone had thought to apply that title to the children of immigrants who lack documentation but are American in every other way that counts.

That's right. Though I am a proud naturalized US citizen now, I was in fact undocumented for a good portion of my life. As a teenager, when I wanted to get a job at McDonald's to earn some walking-around cash, my friend Vic Moore and I simply rode our bikes to the local Social Security Office and DMV and got the necessary SSN and California State driver's license. It was a simpler time, I guess. My birth certificate and passport, however, reflected that I had not yet become a US citizen.

It was only decades later, after I had already graduated from USC, had married my wife, Cathy, earned an MBA from Pepperdine, had been working in a senior financial role at Pepsi, and would be welcoming our first child, Jessica, that circumstances forced me to finally resolve my citizenship status.

In 1988, Pepsi arranged for senior management to travel to London. It was half business trip, half perk where we were encouraged to bring our spouses. We left the United States with no problem and arrived in London, proceeding through customs without a hitch. It wasn't until we arrived back in the States that I reached a decision point and a fork in the road. Border agents waved US citizens through one line and travelers with a foreign passport through another. Cathy instinctively walked through the US line and presented her documents—her blond hair and blue eyes matching her passport photo. She had nothing to declare to customs. But I guess you could say that I had an issue I needed to clear with them, which was long overdue.

When Cathy sensed I was no longer next to her, she looked over her shoulder to see me standing there, frozen, staring at my Mexican-issued passport. It was strange that after all these years together, my citizenship status had never become an issue. But now that it had, I knew that if I was going to continue on my journey, in both my personal life and my career, I would have to take action and become the American I'd always been in my heart.

• • •

By this time, my career was gaining momentum, and I had learned how to live in two worlds. I found I could successfully shift between the immigrant blue-collar world of my parents and the upper circles of corporate America into which I was increasingly succeeding.

I was rising up in the white-collar environs of graduate school and big corporate brands. My bosses saw that I had an ability to get along with almost everyone—or at least I tried to. They recognized I could pull together a team to accomplish the unexpected. But I never felt like an impostor when I returned to the world that I grew up in.

My dad, Eduardo, never was able to achieve this dual identity, something that became painfully—and, in hindsight, hilariously—apparent when he took me on a campus visit to Harvard during my senior year of high school. Believe it or not, I really didn't understand the prestige of the university.

The name Harvard wasn't exactly a frequent topic of conversation among the guys I hung out with in Mexican neighborhoods of South Central L.A., or even around the beaches in Orange County, California. I simply had no frame of reference to imagine that my destiny would lead me anywhere else than to follow in the footsteps of my dad and uncle into a factory or a shop.

I may not have been thinking about college and my future, but thankfully someone else was—my high school college adviser, Mrs. Duckworth. In my junior year, my strong test scores caught her attention, and she sought me out in the school hallways. "Where are you thinking of applying to college?" she asked me. "What's a college?" I replied, in complete honesty.

Wondering how I had gotten this far in school with such cluelessness, she made it her personal project to help me apply to as many colleges as possible. Thanks to her mentoring me through the process, my application and entrance exams were enough to earn me several offers from top colleges.

An admission letter, plus a scholarship offer, arrived from Harvard, accompanied by an all-expenses-paid invitation to visit the campus. My dad and I would travel to Cambridge, Massachusetts, and see what it was all about.

We arrived at the rarefied environs of the campus and were guided into a formal dinner for prospective students who looked like what central casting would imagine Ivy League students should look like.

I vividly remember the sharp contrast we made with my fellow scholarship winners—me with my long surfer-dude hair falling over my polo shirt, which I had tucked into my shorts.

Eduardo was wearing his usual: denim pants, short-sleeved shirt, and his famous large silver retracting key chain that was clipped onto his leather belt. (*Why all those keys?* I still ask myself!)

If I felt uncomfortable, I could only imagine how my dad felt. Like Tio Beto, Eduardo was a union man, but more rank-and-file. We didn't even need to commit the faux pas of not knowing which was the salad fork. It was clear, right off the bat, that this wasn't the place for me.

I look back on that day with sadness and some regret. It's not that I wish I had enrolled, necessarily; but I had left without giving it a try. I had deselected myself simply because I didn't fit in or hail from the same backgrounds as the others. And by leaving, I had guaranteed that there would be at least one fewer person who looked like me in rooms like that.

When we returned from that abortive trip to Cambridge, I put the offers from Harvard, as well as Berkeley, UCLA, and USC, on the back burner. The idea of college just didn't seem urgent to me, especially not after the Harvard visit. No one else I knew went to college. Why should I? Where would it lead me? My indifference to college was born not out of arrogance but out of ignorance. I had not yet discovered this new world, much less learned how to adapt myself to it.

Instead, I spent the months after my high school graduation enjoying a typical and carefree Southern California summer.

Photos from that time are damning evidence of a misspent youth, with my unwieldy shock of hair, bleached a reddish tone by the ocean water, that I kept out of my face with the use of hair ties, borrowed (or stolen) from my sisters. My four wonderful children, wily as ever, relish those photos of me; I suspect they give them excellent leverage on their dad.

This driftwood attitude toward life would have been my destiny, if not for a chance conversation with a surfing buddy of mine. As we paddled in the water, scanning the horizon for another incoming set, my friend told me he was starting college in a few weeks. "Didn't you get a scholarship at SC, Oscar?" he asked me.

He was right, I had. I was about to tell him that I'd decided not to go to college when I thought better of it. Perhaps it was my competitive side expressing itself. *Well, if he's going to college, maybe I should, too,* I thought. Years earlier, Eduardo had moved the family to Santa Ana, which is about an hour's drive from USC's campus.

So I borrowed Dad's car and decided to head to campus on enrollment day. *How complicated could it be to get set up with a few classes?* I thought naïvely.

I arrived on induction day and found my way to the basketball stadium where students were filing into long lines to be admitted. Talk of majors and minors, housing fees, textbook bills, and a host of other costs that I couldn't afford immediately scared me away. I turned on my heel and began walking back to where I'd parked. I needed to get the family car back to Eduardo soon anyhow, or I'd catch hell from him.

As I passed a row of houses—what I would learn was Fraternity Row—I heard someone yell my name. "Hey, Oscar!" I turned to the porch of one of the houses, and there was a guy from the beach whom I had met over the summer, Marco, holding a beer and waving me over.

"All right, so you decided on USC, huh?" he asked, handing me a beer. "Great choice. Where are you living?"

I'd tried to enroll, I explained, but the lines were so long, and the process confused me, so I left. "Maybe I'll come back later," I said, obviously not understanding how this all worked.

"Wait," said Marco, confused. "Aren't you on a scholarship?"

I shrugged. "I think, so, yeah. But that's only for tuition. What about all the other stuff?"

Marco called in another of his fraternity brothers. "This is Brian. He works in the admissions office. He can help."

"Oscar," Brian said to me, laughing at my cluelessness, "enrollment fees, tuition, and books, they're all covered by the scholarship."

I looked at them quizzically. "Are you sure?"

Not relenting, the two of them went over to the phone, dialed a number, and eventually got through to the dean's office, which oversees the scholarship program. "Hello. I think we've got one of your guys here," Brian said into the phone. "Apparently, Oscar got a little overwhelmed and says he's leaving. Did you not get in touch with him yet?"

"We've been trying to contact him for weeks!" said the voice on the other line.

When you live with eight brothers and sisters in a house with a single landline, not all your phone messages reach you. I am sure there's an unopened letter from USC somewhere in Eduardo's attic containing my scholarship offer and instructions for enrollment.

"Bring him here now and we'll get him enrolled," they said. Within twenty minutes, they had me in the dean's office, and with a stroke of the pen, I was suddenly a college student.

Brian and Marco invited me back to the fraternity house to celebrate, but I said I needed to get back home. "You're not living on campus?" they asked. I told them I couldn't afford it.

They offered to let me stay on the couch in the lobby of the house until I saved up enough money and figured things out. It wasn't hard to move in—I didn't have much in the way of a wardrobe.

It didn't seem to matter to any of these fraternity brothers that I came from a very different world from their own, though they eventually needed the couch back. So I found a small room where I could lay out a sleeping bag. Much of my first couple years at USC were spent sleeping on the floor, next to a stack of books and a record player my high school girlfriend gave me. The other guys couldn't believe how I was living, but I couldn't have cared less. I'd slept in worse places; it wasn't anything new to me. I was just happy to feel like I belonged.

The only problem was that the scholarship didn't cover food. Luck struck again when I found a work-study program and got myself hired for a fairly unusual job. The engineering school needed someone to go out to LAX and record the decibel levels of approaching aircraft for an experiment, the object of which I couldn't begin to explain now. As I sat, night after night, underneath the screaming jets of landing airplanes with my 1980s-era recording equipment, I had no idea that this would not be my last job involving airplanes.

In my sophomore year, I felt like I was on a roll. Harvard had called again to see if I'd like to transfer to Cambridge. Tempting as it was, I told them, "No, thanks." I knew I was home. Thank God I didn't take them up on that offer, because a few weeks later I met Cathy, my future wife.

We began to run into each other socially on campus and I figured she was out of my league.

Then, one evening, I went to a party with my best friend, Scott Frisbee—a fraternity brother who had taken me under his wing. I had finally found a place to live with a few of the fraternity guys, but money was tight—so that meant I was still permanently sleeping on the floor. But Scott was my surrogate brother and looked out for me. I am fortunate that he remains a best friend; if he wasn't, I would owe him more than I could repay.

Back then, however, we didn't know what life had in store for us. And at the party, we spotted Cathy and her friend standing across the room. We worked up the courage to approach.

Cathy's friend was pretty vocal about her indecision regarding whom she wanted to take to their annual sorority mixer, Scott or me. Cathy decided to make things easier and said, "Oh, I'll take Oscar!"

It didn't seem to bother her that I was crashing with three fraternity brothers, and—because of meager funds—I was still sleeping on the floor. But when I was around her, I never felt homesick or alone. And for the next thirty years, as long as we were together, I never would.

• • •

Fast-forward to the international arrivals area at LAX International Airport, as Cathy and I reached a crossroads. It was finally time to resolve my immigration status, once and for all.

Cathy and I, along with my mom, Francisca, and Eduardo, my dad, would need to travel to Mexico to locate my original birth and citizen records and deliver them to the US customs and naturalization office. Eduardo, whose last name I had been using in America all those years, was then required to legally adopt me, which he had never done.

"I don't know why I have to adopt my own son," he said, livid. (Note to the reader: I am significantly cleaning up his actual choice of words, a mix of profanity in both Spanish and English.) It had taken a long time, and lots of hard days and heartaches, but Eduardo truly had become my father, both in spirit and now on paper.

I had become a documented immigrant and would become a full American citizen some ten years later, at last a Dreamer no longer.

We welcomed baby Jessica in 1988. Kellie would be born in 1990, followed seven years later by Kevin, and finally by Jack in 2000.

My mother never got to share in many of these joys. The day she died, at the terribly young age of fifty-four, from metastatic breast cancer, I feel like she took part of Eduardo with her. He followed many years later, in 2021. And at Tio Beto's funeral in 2022, hundreds of his union members, past and present, joined our family to say farewell to him.

All family histories are full of mysteries to the younger generation, with elisions and ellipses in the record that hide what our parents didn't necessarily want their children to know about. It's up to the younger generation to try to fit the puzzle pieces together, to better understand and relay the family narrative.

Over the years, my brothers and sisters have compared notes and tried to better understand the choices our parents and grandparents made, and we've tried to pass on these stories so that our own children can understand their identities better. More important, I want them to be able to pass on to their own children a feeling of gratitude for the incredibly fortunate circumstances that allowed our family to thrive in America.

. . .

Allow me to close this chapter the way I began it. Indeed, my life story is a quintessentially American one. It illustrates the immense doors of opportunity that this country is capable of opening to an individual person, like me. It also reminds us of how much a country, company, or community gains when it chooses to open its doors in the most inclusive way possible.

My life is a study in the value, tangible and otherwise, of paving the way for others.

From a dedicated high school counselor who refused to let me give up on my future, to a group of earnest college students who stopped me from walking away on the first day of enrollment and convinced me I belonged.

From Michael Ward, who took a chance in hiring me, even when I wasn't a railroad industry expert yet, to Gordon Bethune, the legendary CEO of Continental, who—along with his successor, Larry Kellner—invited me to serve on the Continental board in 2004.

If there's one lesson from this history of happenstance, it's that people were willing to take chances on me. I just tried to make sure that the colleges, the companies, and the country that bet on my success realized a healthy return on their investment in the end.

The case for greater diversity, equity, and inclusion across our society is clear from a moral standpoint as a matter of fairness. Yet we know the doors of opportunity remain slammed shut for too many people because of what they look like, how they pray, and who they love. We are all the poorer for it.

Bill Norwood, a legend in United Airlines lore and the first African

American pilot in the company's history, put it this way: "Whether it was segregation or discrimination, not only against people of color but also women, we were taught you have to work twice as hard to get half as far."

Surely, he was right, especially in the times in which he lived.

My friend and United board colleague Carolyn Corvi explained what it was like for her as a young woman building an aviation career in the 1970s, when the path to the top was vanishingly narrow and the role models few. "When I think about how I would describe finding my way," she said to me, "it was like walking in a familiar neighborhood in the dark without a flashlight. You sort of know where the landmarks were, but you didn't exactly know where you were going or what may be around the next corner."

I certainly encountered my share of slights, often having to find my own way, especially early in my career. Corporate America was a different place in the eighties and nineties from what it is today, though obviously not different enough. It was a time when it was discouraged to talk about race or ethnicity in the workplace, and the competitive advantage that diversity delivers wasn't appreciated or valued.

When I first began sitting on boards around two decades ago, there certainly weren't a lot of people who looked like me.

The gender parity gaps across C-Suites, boardrooms, and middle management were vastly greater back then, even more so than they are today. Diversity and inclusion initiatives were often regarded as important for morale and corporate reputation, but not a matter of core business management. That is changing, fast.

As evidence of that, in 2021, Nasdaq introduced its Board Diversity Rule for companies that list on its exchange. Nasdaq is responding to its investors who are looking for diverse-run companies to invest in because they know greater diversity is correlated to stronger returns.

You'll recall, I took the job in the first place partly out of a determination to accelerate United's push to attain greater diversity at every level. I was careful to frame it this way, as a matter of competitiveness, strategic advantage, and culture building.

Over the next several years, our board set about diversifying itself, in addition to promoting more women around the E-Team table and throughout our officer corps. I was incredibly proud of the pipeline of talent that we had built to ensure that United would always have a deep bench across the company, one that is diverse and inclusive. We made it a priority to increase diversity on our slates of candidates for job openings at every level. For example, prior to the pandemic, 85 percent of our slates had women on them and we remained determined to further improve on that.

I see the legacy of these actions as I look across the company. Women are not just breaking glass ceilings at United, they're soaring above them, from the corporate offices to the front line to the flight deck itself.

In 2020, United created the new United Aviate Academy, which will train ten thousand new aviators, with the goal that half of them will be women or candidates of color. We are also breaking down another huge barrier to entry—financial costs—so that no financial shortfall prevents an aspiring aviator from reaching her dreams.

Jane Garvey became the first woman to ever lead the board of a major US airline during my tenure. Brett Hart became the first African American to lead a US carrier as president. By the time I retired, United's board of directors had become one of the most diverse in the industry, and our officer corps was on track to reach gender parity.

I'm often asked by board chairs and CEOs how to make their own boards more representative. I advise them to look within their own companies as the best place to find talent to elevate into high-level positions, and that they should reserve at least one or two board seats specifically for rising stars to occupy. Such a person likely has the pulse of the organization, is closer to the product level, and has an intuitive understanding of where the future is trending.

Even when someone still needs a lot more professional career development, that shouldn't be a reason to defer advancement. After all, there's a reason why we call them "future leaders"—they need time, and opportunity, to grow.

United is blessed with a built-in advantage by virtue of being a global operating company, with diversity coded into our DNA. The company draws talent from all over the world, making us stronger and more competitive in the global race for talent.

Our employees hail from countries that span the globe. Per regulations, everyone speaks English, but conversations among employees are quite often inflected with the distinct accents and dialects of the destinations we serve. Even within the Willis Tower, our headquarters/corporate support center, if you walk the hallways, you will hear voices from every corner of our far-flung, polyglot community. At lunchtime, the office cantinas are filled with aromas of the local cuisines that employees bring back from their recent travels, perhaps after visiting family and friends in their home countries.

As CEO, I discovered that this level of diversity placed a higher set of expectations on my leadership. During difficult times, I felt employees increasingly looking to me to speak authentically and directly on key issues and on behalf of many viewpoints, especially at moments of national trauma or upheaval.

At first, I tended to retreat from that responsibility, fearing to alienate or offend one constituency or another. To be fair, United was in such dire straits in my early years as CEO that it felt wise to ensure we remained laser-focused on improving our service and engaging employees, not wading into thorny social and political issues.

There are times, however, when silence becomes a vise, when a company has no choice but to speak out because it finds its values and reputation suddenly on the line.

That was the case in the fall of 2017, when I chose to speak out in defense of the Dreamers, urging the Trump administration to reconsider its opposition to extending the DACA allowances.

Then, in 2018, the administration requested that US airlines assist with its horrific policy to separate children and send them, alone, back to their countries of origin. At that point, there was no question about United's moral obligations or my own. We publicly condemned the policy and refused to have anything to do with it. Witnessing the suffering inflicted upon the most vulnerable, I felt anguish as an immigrant, and even more so as a parent. I felt outrage as a Hispanic, and even more so as an American, seeing my country behave with such intentional cruelty. I felt compelled to take action as a business leader, and even more so as an employee of a company dedicated—as we are—to connecting people and uniting the world.

A statement of protest was not enough. We had a responsibility to use our planes and our people to actively help reconnect family members who had been torn from one another. I credit our employees, especially our corporate responsibility and communications teams, for rapidly forging a partnership with FWD.us, an outstanding nonpartisan organization, to help operate "Flights for Families."

FWD.us helped these children locate family members living in the United States where they could safely stay, and United would help them get there, including providing free flights and helping passengers travel smoothly. Many of these children didn't speak English and had never flown on a plane, which presents a very sensitive challenge. How does a child who has been separated from a parent on the border find a way to locate family members living in a city somewhere else in the United States? Frontline employees are specially trained to identify and assist at-risk people as they travel. Now I was asking our employees to use that training to help protect the most vulnerable people from our own government's policy. By hosting these passengers, we accepted a profound duty of care, and our employees helped so many families become whole again.

On this issue, I simply could not view my role as CEO abstractly, ignoring the fact that I also knew what it means to be separated from one's mother as a young child. *What would have happened to me*, I thought, *if Mama Josefina had not been there to guide me, care for me? What would have happened to us if Tío Beto had not used his resources to help us immigrate? What would have become of me if my dad, Eduardo, had not accepted me into his home and raised me as his own son?*

I had prepared myself, and our employees, to receive a backlash. But none came.

We spoke out and acted in the way we did simply because we could do no other while still doing right by our employees, customers, and stakeholders.

As a sign of the times, we would find ourselves required to engage on pressing issues more often in years to come, from the importance of addressing climate change to battling sexual harassment on our planes.

In 2017, as the world reckoned with the truths of the MeToo movement, I worked with the president of our flight attendant union, Sara Nelson, on an op-ed to support her members and our employees in the skies:

"At United, we know we can't be the company we want and need to be unless we make the best of all our colleagues' energy and skills by promoting diversity and equality throughout our ranks, from our officer corps to the front line."

The message was simple: we aspire to connect the world; therefore we must reflect the world.

Time and again, I found that when I drew upon and applied the lessons that my life taught me, I became a better version of myself and a stronger leader. As leaders seek to make their own organizations more diverse and representative, they will also find themselves asking whether it is right for them to stake a position on an issue.

Sometimes the answer will be yes, and other times, no.

In such moments of uncertainty, the best and perhaps only assurance of getting it right is to have a broad, diverse set of voices to listen to and learn from.

Our decisions are the products of who we are. And that is also true for organizations. The richer, more diverse set of backgrounds that are represented—whether it's in the boardroom or on the shop floor—the stronger and smarter an organization becomes.

It is the job of a leader to cultivate those diverse voices and influences. They heighten awareness within an organization, sharpen decision-making at every level, and deepen the bonds between a brand and its employees and customers.

CHAPTER 12

GAME OF HEARTS

I wondered if I'd ever have the chance to return to Mexico, to again feel the warmth of its sun and the kindness of its people, during those cold and gloomy days in November 2015 as I recovered from the heart attack.

A little more than three weeks had passed since I took that fateful run along the Chicago lakefront. Now, I faced the daunting task of simply learning how to walk again. I still couldn't stand on my own two feet, much less put one of them in front of the other. A few days after the doctors had implanted the LVAD that assisted my heart, the same nurses and orderlies who had so kindly carried me back and forth out of bed so I could look good for the doctors lifted me once more onto a gurney. They strapped me down tightly for the short drive from Northwestern Hospital to the Rehabilitation Institute of Chicago (RIC), which fortunately happened to be ranked as the best physical therapy hospital in the nation.

A medically induced coma withers not only one's skeletal muscle mass; it also ravages one's sense of equilibrium and coordination. I would have to slowly rebuild my ability to perform even the most basic tasks.

Each day, my RIC nurses would knock at my door and take me to physical therapy, a place where you check your ego at the door. I was used to running marathons; now, a shuffle of five feet—before falling into a wheelchair—became a cause for celebration. I also needed to train my right arm, reviving the damaged muscles, tendons, and nerves that had been severed by the fasciotomy surgery.

Standing upright with the support of parallel bars, tossing a beanbag against a wall and managing to catch it, stepping onto a low-rise platform and stepping back down—I took small victories wherever I could get them. But victories paled in comparison to the mighty inspirational triumphs of my fellow patients.

There was one man, a former championship boxer paralyzed in a car crash, who was recovering with me. One day, the physical therapists placed him in a harness that suspended him slightly above a treadmill so he could get the sensation of walking upright for the first time since his accident. From the look of pride and sheer joy in his eyes, you might have thought he was standing on the gold medal platform at the Olympics, or on Everest's summit. I never saw a person stand taller than he did in that moment.

There was another young man, no older than mid-twenties, whose courageous survival from a deadly virus tragically left him a quadruple amputee. Though he had endured a greater share of life's misfortune than I can ever imagine, when I saw him at the hospital's church services no one sang louder or laughed more than he did—his joy at simply being alive seemed more of a divine revelation to me than even the liturgy itself.

I felt humbled to be in the presence of such people, some of the strongest I've ever met in my life.

Their example made it impossible for me to give up on my own progress. Even when I got frustrated, I would see their determination, their stubborn insistence to dictate their own destinies, and I would pick up my exercises where I left off—tossing that beanbag against the wall, shuffling down the hallway, improving with every try. Soon, I was able to walk—haltingly at first, then more smoothly—a few feet at a time, then a few yards, and finally taking laps through the hallways that wrapped around the circumference of the building.

Not without a lot of urging, even begging, I prevailed on my care team to discharge me the day before Thanksgiving. Throughout my recovery at RIC, I couldn't stop recounting the letters that United employees had sent to me, urging me to get better and come back to work.

When Margaret picked me up, I thanked everyone for what they had done for me. The whole family was in the car and we drove straight back to United's headquarters.

Since the Thanksgiving holiday had already begun, most offices were empty. But I wanted to tell people that I was back, or close to it.

There's one floor that's always occupied with people, hard at work, 24/7, 365 days a year.

Cathy, the kids, and I took the elevator up to the Network Operations Center. The team there treated us to a nice lunch, a mini-Thanksgiving—though my appetite was severely limited. As I walked the banks of workstations, fist-bumping with employees and offering my appreciation for their work, I noticed the shock on their faces, as if they'd seen a ghost.

In a sense, they had, because I was essentially a dead man walking. The LVAD kept me alive, but it was far from a substitute for a real heart, and my weak blood circulation left me ashen, gray, and light-headed. The device also required meticulous cleaning around the area where it was inserted into my stomach cavity.

My Northwestern Medicine doctors had given me the news that the LVAD was not a bridge to full recovery; it would have to be a bridge to a heart transplant. I appreciated their diagnosis, but I began setting up appointments with experts around the country, hunting for a second opinion that would tell me what I wanted to hear, that I was fine.

I couldn't find one. The old heart was in a such a state of disrepair that without a healthy transplant, I wouldn't have much life left to live. And that low quality of life was something I wouldn't accept—constant, heavy medications, a sedentary lifestyle, changes in mood and personality.

The consensus was clear. I needed a new heart, soon.

December would be largely devoted to learning the three-dimensional chess game that is required to obtain a heart transplant. The patient, for example, must choose a hospital somewhere in the United States to get on its list for donated hearts that become available. Choose wisely because you must be at that hospital within three hours or risk falling off the list.

I decided to leave Chicago and return to the family home near Jacksonville, Florida, and continued to explore second opinions while also searching for the best options for a hospital. The heart transplant practice in Tampa, Florida, was highly regarded and seemed like the best bet. I could recuperate at home while still being within that three-hour traveling distance should a heart become available.

It was good to finally be back home for a couple of weeks in December, away from the brutal Chicago winter and all the difficult memories it held from those first weeks in the hospital. Then, right before the Christmas holiday, on December 21, Dr. Anderson called to tell me that he'd noticed that the transplant list at Chicago's Northwestern Memorial Hospital was empty. It was the rarest of circumstances, a gift of luck he had rarely if ever encountered. If I transferred back to the Chicago list, I would be the only person on it. We quickly decamped and returned to my tiny two-bedroom apartment in Chicago to celebrate Christmas as best we could. It was a surreal couple of weeks waiting for the call while trying to keep up the holiday spirits.

As onerous as the LVAD was, the thought that my survival now depended on the perishing of a fellow human being weighed heavily on me. I lived in a state of mixed anticipation and anguish, from one moment to the next. I hoped for the sake of my family that we would get that "miracle call" about a heart. A moment later, a wave of dread would wash over me as I realized the price of that gift.

How could it be, I thought, *through the fault of no one, that such a desperate and spiritually fraught decision had been forced on our family?* I kept my ruminations to myself and tried my best to display a brave and encouraging face for the people around me.

Two weeks passed while on the Chicago list. Christmas came and went. Then New Year's, which also came and went, still without any calls. On Sunday afternoon, January 3, my cell phone rang while my wife and I were house hunting north of Chicago. We pulled into a high school parking lot, vacant for the holidays.

I took a deep breath, trying to suppress the lump in my throat, and answered. I was on speakerphone, and I could hear a room full doctors and nurses on the other end.

A person had just passed away, and the heart would be available later that day, they explained. However, there was something they needed me to know about.

I could hear concern in the doctors' voices as they told me the donor was a known drug user and that HIV was a possibility. One doctor piped up to mention that, thanks to antiretroviral treatments, I could still live my life if I contracted HIV/AIDS from the transplant.

I had twenty minutes to make a decision. We hung up and called our most trusted advisers, our kids. We rang our eldest, Jessica, then her sister, Kellie; they had both lived every step of this with us and had really done their homework. It was a tearful call as we weighed our options. We were on the clock, and so we called back the hospital. To buy time, I asked a range of questions. After a few minutes I asked who was next on the list. Would that person take the heart? Without hesitation a nurse spoke up. "The next patient will take it immediately."

That was all I needed to know. "We're going to pass," I said, knowing that with the LVAD I still had time, but that next person on the list clearly didn't. I felt relief, knowing that another person who was in worse condition than me would be saved. But I knew the LVAD wouldn't carry me forever, and the clock was still ticking.

I must admit, focusing on United's future was a welcome respite from thinking about my own.

And, make no mistake, the clock was ticking for United as well. I couldn't control my own future, so I chose to focus on what I could control, the future of United.

To catch up with our competitors and fend off the growing unrest of investors, I needed to lock in on United's go-forward strategy and address our biggest challenges. The original plan had been for the senior UA leaders to meet and assess all the internal reviews that we intended to conduct while I was on my ninety-day listening tour.

Even though things hadn't gone to plan, I wanted to make sure we kept to our schedule. I didn't want to be called in for a transplant and have a crucial strategy meeting take place while I was absent.

So, on Monday, January 4, 2016, the company officers and the executive vice presidents gathered for an off-site retreat. We held the meeting at Chicago's Swissôtel so that we would be removed from the pressures and distractions of headquarters, away from the digital counters on the wall tracking United's D:00, and, also, so that I could have a room upstairs for occasional rests. The LVAD was keeping me quite mobile and energized, but I did tire easily.

It had been more than three months since I had brought in the strategic advisory firm Consequent, led by my friend Jack Bergstrand. His process was aimed at evaluating and strengthening leadership teams, advising them on how to assess the capabilities of individual members and to tie them together to move forward in a unified way. The senior leaders who took part in this advisory process had used those three months well, carefully and honestly evaluating their own strengths and one another's—each arriving at a clearer understanding of their "knowledge of contribution."

Business leaders, so accomplished in their field that they earned their place around the executive table of a major airline, are not accustomed to such self-reflection and inward criticism, and I was impressed with how thoroughly they had embraced the exercise.

They had accepted the fact that, indeed, we had been wandering in different directions, each of them pursuing their own course, guided by their individual lights. I wanted us to locate our north star and align the efforts of every aspect of the company toward a unified guiding principle.

I knew that the other members of the team each had different ideas about what should take priority and orient our turnaround strategy, and three would be the most decisive swing votes—Greg Hart, the head of operations; Linda Jojo, our chief information officer; and Gerry Laderman, acting chief financial officer. Of course, there were many other key leaders with similar focus and intensity on their functional areas, but I knew that the three of them would be the biggest influencers.

With respect to Greg, I had been in his chair at CSX, running the operation. Therefore, I completely understood that he would argue that operations should be our sole focus: "Nothing can arrive before that." That would require a large capital expenditure for planes and other assets that keep our operation humming reliably.

I knew Linda would argue forcefully for investing in better technology and digital capabilities as our top priority. It was essential that our IT systems and our physical systems not just work in harmony but become a fine-tuned machine.

Surely Gerry would argue that our number one goal ought to be tightly managing costs and maintaining profit margins.

For my part, ever since my first weeks on the job, I firmly believed that even with all the other fires burning, we needed to put employees first in our strategy, and that should serve as our north star.

I don't believe in forcing a consensus, which—after all—is a contradiction in terms. Sure, as CEO I could dictate the outcome of our discussions, as those who had sat in my chair previously had done. But if we went ahead with this new strategy, still disunited as an executive team, it would become plain for all to see—investors, competitors, customers, the media, and employees.

I set a ground rule: whichever direction we chose, it would have to be unanimous.

I wanted to win the argument by merits and convince my team that my direction was the correct one, but I was willing to listen and be persuaded. If Greg's operations team was convinced that our number one priority should be growing our routes and schedules and buying new aircraft, then I wanted to hear the case for that. If Linda argued that we should focus primarily on integrating the IT systems, I knew there was a lot of evidence to support that position. Equally, if Gerry's financial team believed that boosting our stock and ratings on Wall Street ought to be the first in a sequence of efforts to turn around the company, I was ready to be convinced.

Throughout that first day, Monday, the team wrestled with the options, decisions, and messages that would emerge from this meeting. We felt the eyes and the anxieties of employees, Wall Street, the board of directors, partners, unions, and passengers on us. We split off into breakout sessions. We made progress and we had setbacks. On the first night, we gathered at a local restaurant, and Brett gave a little speech. The world will little note or long remember what he said, but I'll never forget how his words made me feel. Or, as the poet Maya Angelou famously said, "people will forget what you said, people will forget what you did, but people will never forget how you made them feel." Brett's words reminded me of how much I owed to this group.

Throughout the debates, I would glance at my phone to see if I missed a call from Dr. Anderson. He advised me to stay in the right mental place to go into surgery, given that another transplant might become available at any time. I didn't get my hopes up since we had an appointment scheduled for later in the week, and I was anticipating that we would decide to drop my name off the Chicago heart transplant waiting list and go back to the Tampa list.

The next morning, January 5—my birthday, as it happened—the United staff would regroup for a last discussion that would lead to a final decision from the team.

Dr. Anderson called again.

"Oscar," he said buoyantly, "I've got a kick-ass heart for you. Stay relaxed—but get over here this afternoon and Dr. Pham will operate this evening."

As I hung up the phone, I couldn't stop thinking about the meaning that lay behind Dr. Anderson's words.

A fellow human being, someone with whom I shared this common space of earth and a brief breath of life, had passed away. I knew little about him at the time and it is highly unlikely our paths ever would have crossed.

Yet, in hours, we would find ourselves forever connected in a way that is hard to describe and impossible to fully comprehend.

My life still hung in the balance, but his had expired. I could write volumes about this person and how I think about our interconnectedness. But, out of respect, I don't speak about it—and in the spaces between these lines, what I don't say relates volumes; there are simply no words to capture my indebtedness. And in that deliberate silence, my gratitude and respect are contained.

It was still early in the morning and Dr. Anderson had advised me to take the day off and not let my mind race about the operation. I couldn't do that because, one way or another, this would be my last day at work for a while. If the transplant went well and my body accepted the new heart, then I might be back quite soon. If it didn't, this would be my final act as CEO.

It was therefore vital that we arrived at a unanimous consensus before I left, and equally important that it happened organically. If my team simply backed my view because I was the boss, then our new direction wouldn't survive me.

When I returned to our meeting rooms, I pulled Kate and Brett aside to share the confidential news. It wasn't celebratory—far from it—but they needed to begin planning for my absence. I will never forget the look on Brett's face when he heard the news that I would be out again, this time for a heart transplant—"Mr. Cool" breaking his calm demeanor once more. He would have to continue as interim CEO for another round.

I told them I'd continue with the strategy meeting until noon, when I'd head over to the hospital. No one else was to know.

With the clock ticking toward noon, Linda, Gerry, and Greg moved to a position I had hoped they would reach. I began to notice a growing sense of collaboration, more unity, and increased momentum. The group had coalesced around the working theory that United simply could not achieve the humming operations we needed without the heads and hearts of United employees. Improving our operational reliability as well as investing in our IT systems would be necessary for our turnaround, but not sufficient—not unless we had our employees with us.

As the group consolidated behind this theory of the case, our debate became clearer and stronger—one point refined and sharpened by a counterpoint—until we had arrived at a tentative agreement.

Whatever happened, the senior leaders of the company would return to their respective teams, communicating with a single voice, aligned to a straightforward mandate: "Regain the trust of our employees."

I knew that my "employee-first" strategy would trigger a harsh reaction on Wall Street.

"What the hell do you mean you're investing in your employees?"

"How will that boost your stock?"

As a financial guy, I understood that perspective. Employee morale doesn't fit nicely onto an analyst's spreadsheet. A strategy that put employees first, and customers at the center of everything we do, isn't something investors can easily evaluate. Plus, they'd been waiting for improved results for a few years by this point, and my recent interactions with Brad Gerstner were emblematic of their growing impatience. Soon, it would all spill into a public back-and-forth.

Yet the experiences I had gone through those past months had given me a sense of clarity and resolve. The suffering I heard in the voices of employees during the listening tour, the hope contained in those mailbag sessions from the same employees, the teamwork of so many of my colleagues who had taken extra burdens upon themselves when I was sick—all of it had informed my thinking.

Now, all that was left was for me to go around the table and ask for a show of hands. As the hands began to rise around the table, and the "ayes" tallied, we knew that, if nothing else, we had arrived at this destination as a unified team.

As the final "aye" faded in the room, there was a calm silence, and I breathed a sigh of relief. I locked eyes with Kate, then Brett, and knew it was time to keep my appointment with Dr. Anderson and Dr. Pham.

Soon, the game of hearts that I had been playing for months would come to an end, one way or another. Oddly, despite the risks involved, I felt a deep sense of calm.

I had just pushed my chips to go "all in" on investing in our employees, which was the gamble that meant the most to me. If this was to be the moment where I would stand my ground and be judged as CEO, I was at peace with that. In fact, I welcomed it.

I slid my chair out from the table and stood up, as if I was Doyle Brunson at the World Series of Poker. "Folks, thank you very much. I'm going to head back to the hospital for . . . something we've been waiting for," I explained, hoping they didn't guess what was about to happen. "I'll see you on the other side."

On my way out, I had one final conversation with Brett and Kate. Brett was already working with his team in the general counsel's office to draft a press release and begin informing the board about the impending operation. My new heart, which was being readied as we spoke, wasn't going to wait on the board to give their approval. But obviously we all understood the tension and controversy that exist between the right to privacy, the desire to protect patient confidentiality, and the need for disclosure to shareholders and the media when a CEO's health is in question.

Any news, good or bad, could easily move financial markets. Had there been an obvious successor to me, the stakes might not have been as high. Inaccurate stories might spook investors and hurt the company, maybe even costing my employees their paychecks or jobs. I couldn't allow that to happen, especially when United's situation remained nearly as dire as my own.

Brett told me that they would inform the press and shareholders the following day. By that time, we would know if the transplant had been successful . . . or if it hadn't been.

I made a call to our chairman, Henry Meyer. I wanted him to hear my voice one more time and know that I was confident things would be all right. I understood the difficult situation my health crisis had placed him in; he was receiving pressure from investors and fellow board members who felt like, "Hey, we took a chance on this guy. He came from outside the industry. He's already taken months off for a heart attack. Now, he's going in for a transplant?" I owed Henry one more conversation, and he wished me luck.

Later that evening, I was wheeled into the operating room to the rhythm of my favorite rock band, the Rolling Stones. "You can't always get what you want. But if you try sometimes, you just might find, you get what you need." It's an upbeat tune with a melancholy underside. That seemed about right. My family waited in the lobby for updates as the ten-hour procedure progressed. I would later learn that, since the availability of organs is unpredictable, Dr. Pham would wind up performing three heart transplants in the following days, back-to-back. If I throw around the word "miracle" too much in this book, it's only because people like Dr. Pham—also now a lifelong friend—and my entire medical team seemed to never stop performing them.

I woke up the next morning. I was in a lot of pain, but I woke up. I had a new heart, a new lease on life.

I opened my eyes and saw the family, once again, standing there—joined by other well-wishers from the hospital staff. The first awakening from the medically induced coma was frightening, unsettling, even. This time, by contrast, it was a joyous moment, unalloyed, one that matched the spirit of a new year that had only just begun.

Later that night, I awoke suddenly to find Jessica sitting at my hospital bedside, just like in the first weeks after the initial heart attack. True to form, she had once again deputized herself as the family's medical expert, staying up all night with me. Each time the pain startled me awake, she would generously press that "magic button" that delivered a boost of morphine through my IV.

I could scarcely believe that it had been only a few months since her wedding day, since my heart attack, and since I took the job at United.

I remember wanting to say something to her—what it was I now can't for the life of me remember—but it felt important. Maybe it was to tell her I would be okay. Or maybe something about our family, about how proud her mom and I were of her, Kellie, Kevin, and Jack. Or maybe I wanted to tell her something about her grandmother, or great-grandmother, and how we owed our lives in America to them.

"Shhhh," Jessica said as she pressed the button again. "Go back to sleep, Dad."

Several days later, on January 15, I left the hospital to recuperate at home.

· · ·

As I think back on what transpired during those initial thirty-seven minutes—between the time when I called 911 and when I started to receive life support, as well as the time between when I was placed on the transplant list and when I received the call that a match had been found— it's hard not to believe in miracles.

So many stars had to align for me to be here today, alive on the "other side." The EMTs just happened to be only a block away when they received the emergency call about the initial heart attack. Their ambulance, unlike so many in our country, was a modern one, fitted out with the latest technology as well as the systems to communicate in real time with the doctors at the hospital. In fact, Dr. Flaherty and his colleague were in prep for a routine surgery when they received notice of my imminent arrival and they pivoted immediately so they could treat me. To this day, Flaherty tells me, flatly, that he did not think I would survive. "C'mon," I'll kid him, "I couldn't have been as bad as you let on." "No, Oscar," he'll reply, "you were worse than you will ever realize."

My survival certainly feels miraculous, right down to the fact that I received the gift of a new heart and a second chance at life on my birthday. Perhaps it was divine intervention, I don't know. What I do know is that I am alive thanks to intervention by angels with human hands and heroic hearts, outstanding emergency responders, dedicated and compassionate nurses, and some of the greatest minds in medicine.

Truly, their work was nothing short of divine, as was the gift of a heart, for which I can never truly express sufficient gratitude.

. . .

Our annual leadership meeting was taking place a couple of weeks following the transplant operation. Thousands of senior United global employees and leaders would gather in Chicago to learn of our new direction—I had to be there. News of my recent impromptu visit to the NOC, after I'd left the physical rehab hospital, sent rumors swirling about the reality of my condition. I needed to quiet the speculation and let people get a look at me, from concerned employees to skeptical board members.

I was taking drugs that suppressed my immune system to prevent it from rejecting the new organ, and so Kate and Sonja tried to devise a protocol to keep me safe. They stocked up on hand sanitizer and Clorox wipes (long before COVID, when it became fashionable).

And they suggested that instead of shaking hands, I should fist-bump. "And don't let anyone hug you, Oscar!" they said, repeating Dr. Anderson's strict instructions.

Margaret dropped me off at a rear entrance and I navigated through a maze of service hallways, through the kitchen, walking toward the convention hall. Kate had made sure I would be a surprise addition to the agenda. When I entered the vast event space, people's surprise at seeing me elicited an audible gasp.

The stunned faces of more than two thousand colleagues gave way to a standing ovation, which thankfully lasted for a while so I could compose myself and take a sip of water.

I fumbled for my thoughts. I suddenly realized that almost no one at the company had seen me since before the heart attack. In fact, despite my listening tour, most employees hadn't seen me at all. I looked gaunt, having lost so much weight over the previous three months. My suit hung limply over my shoulders, like clothes over a wire hanger.

During my week of post-op recovery, I had sketched an outline of what I might say. I took a deep breath and told everyone I was excited to get back to what we started.

I thanked everyone for their love and kindness. I told them about the "daily reading" and how much the letters and votives of support meant to my family and to me personally. I told stories from the road, about what our frontline colleagues had told me—Jenna and Amy, the teams in Houston, L.A., Newark, San Francisco, and many others.

"Listen, learn, and only then lead," I said. "That is what I set out to do when I first joined this United family." After a very long journey of listening, it was time to start leading and to cease wandering like nomads in the desert.

I explained how the reorganization and alignment of our executive strategy into the "E-Team" provided an example, in microcosm, of the kind of unification that we needed to achieve across our operation. We need to find our north star and always follow that.

"The morning of my heart transplant," I said, "the E-Team and I agreed during an offsite that our north star must be you, all of us, the people of United Airlines.

"We must earn the trust of every employee, and that trust must cascade throughout the organization and to our customers. And we must move toward a more meritocratic system, a culture that puts the best leaders in place. We need to move beyond the era of sub-Con and sub-UA and start flying together.

"There is so much to do to better serve our passengers, but we can only do those things together, United."

The applause line achieved the desired result. As I walked offstage, the emotional high would prove short-lived, unfortunately.

A fuse had been lit on a shareholder coup that had been brewing among a group of dissident investors and would come close to sparking a full-scale proxy battle that, in my opinion, would've unraveled everything we were aiming to achieve.

CHAPTER 13

A UNITED FRONT TO A PROXY FIGHT

On April 6, 2016, United celebrated its ninetieth anniversary.

"To mark this historic occasion," read the message that was sent out to all airline union members by their leadership, "United Flight Attendants will picket with pilots and other employees."

They showed up, in force, at One International Place in Boston's Financial District, outside the offices of two investment funds that held a significant stake in United—PAR Capital and Altimeter Capital.

The protest began at 11:00 a.m. sharp. If you were an office worker stepping out for lunch on that early spring day, you may have seen the airline workers marching in the streets and wondered, "Another example of disunity at United?"

Not quite.

They held signs with slogans like:

UNITED AIRLINES WILL CLIMB WITHOUT ALTIMETER.

NOT "PAR" FOR UNITED'S COURSE.

HOSTILE HEDGE FUNDS: LET OSCAR DO HIS JOB!

Perhaps for the first time in our company's ninety-year history, unionized employees were picketing in *support* of United, its chief executive, and leadership, not against it. Instead, the heads of our major unions had rallied their members against these two investment funds that were trying to assume control of our board so they could steer the company in a way that I believed would be detrimental for United and its employees.

At the time, United's employee base had risen to nearly eighty-five thousand, with close to 90 percent being union represented. Both United and American Airlines are heavily unionized, while at Delta only the pilots are represented.

The spirit of solidarity on display at that protest in Boston—however limited—marked a sharp departure from the acrimony that had soured relations between management and labor ever since the merger.

For example, at the June 2015 shareholders meeting, the International Brotherhood of Teamsters, who represent United's maintenance technicians, picketed outside the Willis Tower. Meanwhile, inside the shareholders meeting, United's senior leaders at the time abruptly ended the customary question-and-answer session, cutting off the Teamsters' leader while he was speaking—a demonstration of disrespect in front of investors, the public, and our employees. If you've ever attended a shareholders meeting (and I assume most people haven't), you would know that this is not the way to do business.

And just a month later, in July 2015, union unrest was on public display again when Sara Nelson, president of the Association of Flight Attendants (AFA), called for a worldwide protest against United. "Enough is enough," said Sara. "Flight attendants have given a lot to United Airlines, and we deserve a fair contract in return."

Yet, by the following April, just nine months after the demonstrations that saw more than two thousand flight attendants protesting in airports across the globe, the union members were suddenly on our side (protesting outside PAR's and Altimeter's offices)—*despite* the fact that we still hadn't finalized contracts for flight attendants or for most of our other union employees. This was a welcome surprise.

The episode that follows was just one of the many challenges that United faced, in what turned out to be a battle on multiple fronts—all occurring at roughly the same time.

• • •

As I explained at the start of this book, my relationship with Brad Gerstner's investment firm and the unions intersected on the morning of my heart attack.

By a sheer scheduling coincidence, I was set to interview a potential CFO at the behest of Brad. Then we'd planned to conduct our first-ever labor summit with union leaders. As the cardiac interventionist aspirated the blood clot from my heart and placed me on life support, the union bosses, as well as Brad's candidate, were left scratching their heads as to what had happened to me. Of course, they would find out the following day when the news broke in the media.

Oddly, these parallel stories would intersect again as I sought to simultaneously defuse a potential proxy battle while bringing our long-awaited labor negotiations in for a landing.

Perhaps it was fated that these two issues would go hand in hand. While I was on sick leave, our labor relations team, led by Mike Bonds and Doug McKeen, continued with our negotiations. I had insisted on the following: We recalibrate our approach to these negotiations. We tone down the adversarial relationship. We don't give away the farm, by any means, but recognize that our union brethren were indeed family and we needed to work together.

I believe that my health crisis actually helped this process along. Everyone knew that this was my priority, and I wouldn't want my health crisis to become an excuse for progress to stall, even for a moment.

While I was in the hospital, Brad's firm, Altimeter, as well as PAR Capital, which was run by Paul Reeder, another investment fund with an investment in UAL, sent letters to Henry Meyer, our board chair, suggesting alternative CEO candidates should I not be able to return.

I didn't take offense at the move. After all, it was a valid point to make, which is why the board hired an independent third-party medical consultant to advise on my condition. I granted permission for my doctors to brief the consultants, who then explained in lay terms to the board exactly what was happening with me so they could make the most responsible choices for the company.

Then, in late January, they raised the stakes.

While I was at home recovering from the transplant operation, Altimeter and PAR made big news by filing a Schedule 13D with the US Securities and Exchange Commission (SEC), which means they were now working together as an activist group. Together, they now owned a combined 7.1 percent of United's outstanding shares. This was Brad and Paul's way of firing a shot across our bow, indicating that they were serious about launching a full-scale campaign with the goal of making significant changes to the makeup of our board.

The game was on, and I would have to get us geared up for it.

• • •

I hadn't returned full-time yet, but my apartment in Chicago had become a satellite office of the E-Team—where I took meetings, interviewed people for important positions that I still needed to fill, and set the groundwork for my return. While I kept an eye on developments on the investor front, my attention was focused on what was happening with respect to the union negotiations that were taking place a few blocks down the street at the historic Palmer House Hotel on Michigan Avenue.

We had rented out nearly all the conference rooms on the basement level of the beautiful Chicago landmark, each one occupied by either United's labor relations team or the negotiating teams of each of our unions. The scene sort of resembled an NFL draft, with each union setting up its own war room along the row of conference suites that lined a single corridor. United's labor relations team had its own command center in the same hallway. For several months, the place would become a hub of activity, as our negotiators carried on simultaneous discussions with each union.

Emotions ran high in those gilded rooms, which quickly took on a distinctive hothouse atmosphere, with lots of people crammed together under stressful conditions for long stretches of time.

At first, the odds of success appeared very slim. From an investor perspective, the "smart money" was to bet on the likelihood that the same issues that had divided the airline and the unions ever since the merger would poison any chance for a mutually beneficial agreement.

We had successes and setbacks. Our team would spend weeks hammering out the fine points of these deals, patiently pushing each boulder up the hill. Sometimes, the boulder would roll back down the hill and we'd have to start over. Other times, we got lucky and managed to strike deals that proved the skeptics wrong, and sometimes even surprised us.

Then, in late January—the same week that Brad and Paul formed their investor group—we struck a deal with the pilots' union, the Air Line Pilots Association (ALPA). Led by Jay Heppner, who was also a career United pilot, ALPA agreed to a two-year extension of its contract. It was a big win and it established precedent that we could get things done, that progress wasn't impossible.

This victory generated momentum, and our team continued to make headway with the unions representing our other major work groups. However, the relationship with our flight attendants' union had deteriorated to the point that we were barely on speaking terms.

The problem of "common metal" remained. That is, legacy United and legacy Continental crews were contractually disallowed from working together on the same aircraft—common metal—until a joint contract was reached. As I've explained, this situation led to many delays and flight cancellations and perpetuated the us-versus-them mentality between the two groups.

Naturally, this made our customers unhappy—creating yet another issue to solve. It also made flight attendants deeply unhappy, which I saw firsthand every place I traveled.

When Amy, the flight attendant I spoke with during my listening tour, had told me that she spent her entire workday apologizing to customers about a million problems outside her control, she spoke for all her colleagues. That sense of unfairness needed to be acknowledged before our negotiations could proceed in a mutually respectful way.

The flight attendants felt (rightly) that the burdens of the stalled merger had fallen heavily on their shoulders, as nearly all in-person complaints are directed toward them. They are the face of our service in the minds of most customers.

Think about it. When you have a problem with your seat assignment on the plane, you don't call up the gate agent who assigned you, do you? Of course not. You complain to the flight attendant. If your plane is stuck on the tarmac waiting for a replacement part, you don't complain to the maintenance team or to the pilot. Many of these inefficiencies stemmed from the failure to integrate and there was a growing sense among our United flight attendants that they were having to make up for the failings of the merger, poisoning relations. It *had* to be fixed.

However, by February 2016, we were approaching six years since the merger, still with no contract covering flight attendants—still with no common metal. The AFA president, Sara Nelson, was stepping up her rhetoric, driving our negotiating teams farther apart.

I didn't know Sara well, and I'd hoped that the labor summit we'd planned to take place in October 2015 would give me a chance to build a rapport with her—and, importantly, to listen. But the heart attack canceled that opportunity.

Thankfully, by early February 2016, as I was recovering from the transplant, Jay Heppner of the pilots' union generously volunteered to help arrange a friendly "get-to-know-you" meeting between Sara and myself. I don't know exactly what Jay said to her. But our negotiations with ALPA had been positive. Based on the strength of that experience, his message to her was: "This guy is different."

Sara would judge that for herself, to be sure. A force of nature on behalf of her members, Sara would later be dubbed "The World's Most Powerful

Flight Attendant" in a profile by the *New York Times*, and she had built a reputation that is both admired and respected in the power corridors of Washington, DC.

I must admit, I walked into the meeting with my guard up. I was protective of our team and I felt they didn't deserve some of the harsh criticism that I'd heard from the AFA and from Sara herself. Having said that, I went into the meeting ready to have a constructive discussion and to really understand the issues that needed to be resolved.

I doubt Sara held great optimism that my arrival as CEO would change the dynamic. I knew that many of the conversations I was having with her members during my listening tour had reached her ears, but she probably dismissed them as more empty talk from management.

Sara was a United Airlines flight attendant, and so I started our discussion by simply asking how she had gotten into union leadership from the start. I truly wanted to understand her perspective so that I could figure out how to begin to fix United's relations with Sara's union members.

After graduating from college with a teaching degree, she explained to me, she moved to St. Louis and found herself juggling four jobs just to keep her head above water. In the depths of a particularly cold Missouri winter, her friend who had just become a flight attendant rang her from Miami. Sara listened as her friend described the career path—the flexibility, good pay and benefits, as well as the excitement and adventure. Sara was convinced. She packed up her car and drove to Chicago to interview at United. Six weeks of training later, she was crewing her first flight out of Boston.

The industry that Sara joined back in 1996 was a very different one from today's and so much of that progress is thanks to the brave work of Sara and her colleagues, on many fronts but not least with respect to combating the outrageous double standards applied to women, as well as the intolerable sexism and harassment from customers that ran rampant.

Many of the seniority rules also worked against younger applicants who wanted to become flight attendants, and Sara found that out the hard way. She wouldn't receive a paycheck until she had completed enough routes, which is hard for a new hire because they're at the back of the line. Living off spare meals from the galley during flights, one day she arrived back to her flight attendant domicile after working back-to-back shifts and checked her bank account. It was zero, and her first paycheck was still days away. Just as she was beginning to lose hope, someone wearing a United uniform tapped her on a shoulder. The flight attendant asked Sara how to spell her name and then wrote out an $800 check. She handed it to Sara and said, "First, go and take care of yourself. And number two, call our union."

"I learned everything I needed to know about our union in that moment," Sara said to me, beginning to choke up. "Because in our union, we take care of each other and we're never alone."

Sometime later, she told me that the day we'd had lunch was actually her twentieth anniversary as a United flight attendant. It had completely slipped her mind.

Sara understood what her members go through every day because she lived that life and, in fact, continues to serve on United flight crews to keep her membership in good standing. She reminded me of the very best labor leaders I had worked with over my career.

That meeting would prove decisive, not only in our efforts to strike a fair deal for our flight attendants but also in the battle with Altimeter and PAR.

• • •

In late February, a couple of weeks after my meeting with Sara, it was time to meet with Brad Gerstner and Paul Reeder, face-to-face, and clarify their intentions.

As a venue for the meeting, we chose the offices of a local Chicago law firm—neutral territory.

I arrived, flanked by Brett Hart, who was still in place as interim CEO, as well as David Vitale, a board member. Before we met as a group, Brad asked that I meet with Paul and him privately.

I suspect that this first private session was meant for them to lay eyes on me so they could make their own judgment about my mental acuity and health. Though still much skinnier than usual, I apparently looked healthy enough and passed their test. They did not suggest any immediate calls for me to step down and, in fact, would later publicly support me as CEO.

I acknowledged that they held valid concerns about United's leadership and about me personally. True, I was a railroad guy by experience, not a commercial aviation guy. I gently reminded them, however, that I had a track record at CSX. I'd proven that I knew how to run a complex operating company with sophisticated logistical concerns and long-lived, capital-intensive assets—not to mention, I had built a reputation for winning the trust of unions. I acknowledged that it wasn't optimal for the new CEO of a company in a turnaround situation to step away for an extended period for health reasons. But I was feeling healthy and energized, ready to jump into the fray.

I also cautioned them by offering some advice derived from hard-won experience. If they believed United's problems could be solved by simply swapping in some new executives, even at the very top, they were mistaken. The problems were deeper than that; I needed more time to fully develop and execute a strategy, as well as to get buy-in from my leadership team and the unions.

We then adjourned into a larger conference room. Brett, David, and I—along with our lawyers—sat on one side of the conference table, with Brad and Paul on the other. Brad explained that they were fine with me remaining at my post, but Altimeter and PAR wanted board seats, a new chairman, and some say in the hiring of strategic and financial executives who could make United more competitive and produce a better return on their investment.

Then they dropped the bombshell. They wanted us to install Gordon Bethune, the legendary airline executive who had led Continental to new heights as CEO, as chairman of the board.

I saw the look on both Brett's and David's faces, and I am sure they registered the look on mine. When I heard Gordon's name, I instantly knew that this conversation had scaled up into an even more serious and complex situation.

Gordon was, and will always remain, a friend. He was the one who recruited me to join the Continental board in 2004. I was the youngest member of the board then, and the opportunity was pivotal in my career. I had no plans to get caught in a messy public fight with someone who is both a mentor and one of the most revered figures in our industry.

Nevertheless, I knew that his presence on the board would deepen the already widening divisions between the legacy United employees and legacy Continental at precisely the moment when I was trying to bring people together. The cultures needed to be merged and unified—with a shared common goal, whereby all employees could benefit.

During Gordon's time at the helm of Continental, Houston had been the center of the universe. His return as chairman would signal to the entire company that Continental and its legacy employees were now running the show. The employees from United weren't going to accept that outcome under any circumstance. It was a deal breaker for half of my employees; therefore, it was a nonstarter for me.

The two sides now understood each other's positions, and the ultimatum from the investor side to United was clear. Either I accepted their proposal willingly or they would take the matter directly to shareholders in a public vote, forcing us into a proxy battle.

We left the meeting and, like boxers returning to their corners to wait for the bell to ring, both sides began preparing themselves for the fight to come.

Fortunately, I had thought ahead. In an adjoining conference room, an assembled team was already waiting for me, led by Eduardo Mestre, senior managing director and chairman of global advisory at Evercore, who had been one of my field generals during a previous proxy battle, at CSX in 2008. I explained to them what Brad had just told me about their intentions, and we would have to get our battle plans ready.

While they got to work, so did I. I began working the phones to shore up support from our institutional investors. I also began actively recruiting new directors to add to the board.

Eduardo's team, as well as Brett Hart's, began to exchange offers and counteroffers with the investment funds.

To their credit, Altimeter and PAR came back to us with a reduced ask, revising their request for a slate of six proposed seats down to five, which they then reduced to three seats. Finally, they offered to accept just two seats. Yet, with each offer, they stuck to their guns and insisted that Gordon had to be named chairman. We countered by accepting their offer of two seats, and even suggested that Gordon could be named as a director. But I held firm that Gordon couldn't be chairman.

We were at an impasse. But this period of negotiation had given our team valuable time to develop a defense strategy and we were now ready to implement it. The first step was announcing the slate of board members we had recruited and vetted.

The stage was set for more drama, which would play out in Houston, Gordon's home turf and the base of his most ardent support.

CHAPTER 14

SHOWDOWN IN HOUSTON

On Sunday, March 6, 2016, I issued a message to employees and shareholders that I would formally return to work full-time on March 14, though I had been working from my apartment since I returned from the hospital in January. The next day, I took a flight to our hub in Houston, where we had scheduled three massive town hall meetings with each of our work groups at the airport.

The news that Gordon might potentially return would send shock waves throughout the Houston-based Continental employees, many of whom longed for the days when he had led the company. United employees, on hearing the news, would feel that the rug had just been pulled out from under them. After all this talk of being on the same team, it would signal that one side had won, likely making permanent the divisions that I was trying to heal.

I needed to act first to prevent this powder keg from exploding. It was my job to try to explain to employees what all of this meant, to assure them that I was determined to fight this thing to the end, come what may.

When I landed, we were ready to announce our own nominations to the board, including two industry insiders. I made my way to the ballroom of the airport Marriott, where thousands of Houston employees were waiting to hear me speak. It felt like entering the lion's den.

Along the way, I called Brad to tell him what was about to happen. There was no doubt that our board nominees had unimpeachable business credentials and experience, exactly what Brad had originally said that he wanted. But that wasn't what he wanted to hear.

He tried to convince me to hold off, assuring me that, as the new chairman of the board, Gordon would provide outstanding advice and guidance. I didn't disagree with this fundamental premise, but I knew that the solution to the core issues at hand was not something that Gordon could solve. I told Brad flatly, "You have our answer. Now, we need to decide how we manage this process without further dividing our company."

Our press release dropped at nearly the same moment that I took the stage. The atmosphere among the hundreds of employees was heated, verging on hostile. For hours on end, I took questions from the crowd as employees waited in lines for their chance to express years of pent-up frustration.

As it became clear that I wasn't going to lose my temper or shut anyone down, the gale force of emotion abated; slowly but surely, the temperature in the room fell and the mood became conversational rather than confrontational. At the end of each town hall, employees who had been yelling at me only minutes before would approach, eager to take photos and shake hands. I was still immunocompromised, and my right hand still hurt like hell when I shook hands because of the fasciotomy surgery.

But every hand I shook felt like a win, and a genuine ear-to-ear smile on my face masked the pain from each grip. It was worth it.

The next day, March 8, with more town halls on the docket, Brad and Paul struck back. They announced their own slate of candidates, now revised back up to the original six, including Gordon. Their press release was accompanied by an open letter to UAL, signed by Brad and Paul, attacking us in heated, highly personalized terms.

"Your seemingly desperate actions yesterday appear as a transparent and cynical attempt to maintain your official privileges and power," they wrote, "despite your long historical record of deficient oversight on behalf of stockholders."

It was incendiary, and it lit up the media with speculation about United's future, and mine.

Fortunately, I had backup.

Todd Insler, who took over from Jay Heppner as the pilots' representative on the board, saw what was happening, disagreed with what the activist investors were attempting, and decided to do something about it. While I was speaking to employees in the ballroom downstairs at the Marriott, Todd and the leadership of the pilots' union were huddled in a room upstairs, crafting a rebuttal statement.

In between town hall sessions, I popped up to the hotel room where they were working to see how it was coming.

"We are concerned that these activists will instigate a program focusing on short-term gains to the detriment of United's customers and employees," he wrote. "Our returning CEO, Mr. Oscar Munoz, has renewed hope in our pilots through his genuine belief in our product and our people. The pilots of United Airlines share his vision and fully support Mr. Munoz. We will work with him to reestablish United Airlines as the industry leader."

This message went public the same day that Brad and Paul issued their letter. Then, within hours, Sara Nelson released her own statement.

"Oscar Munoz has presented a vision for United Airlines that passengers and employees can believe in," she wrote, adding that "these investors are creating a distraction at just the wrong time if their interest is truly in turning around United and building an airline that will again lead the industry with performance, profits, share price and, importantly, engaged employees who take pride in the place where they work."

The machinists' union—whom Brett had been addressing from O'Hare when I saw him on television that day in the hospital—issued a statement of support as well.

This united front was certainly not what PAR and Altimeter had expected when they launched this campaign. The forcefulness of the unions' support surprised even me.

· · ·

"It's not a way to welcome someone back, I guess," Carl Quintanilla said to his fellow CNBC host Jim Cramer as the battle of words mounted.

I didn't share that feeling, strangely. The hardball tactics and harsh words from the activists weren't the headlines I wanted as I returned to the job, of course—far from it.

But the attacks directed by the investors toward United succeeded in unifying us, perhaps better than any words of mine could have.

In a moment of need, our union partners and employees rode to the rescue.

They could have easily sat on the sidelines, waiting to see which side would prevail. But they didn't. Their words left no daylight between labor and management, and they left me speechless.

What better welcome back could I ask for?

I had demonstrated my willingness to address Brad's concerns by recruiting more airline experience to the board. Plus, the combination of employees and unions who were rallying behind me was enough to restart our discussions with Brad and Paul on a more even keel.

A few days after my visit to Houston, I spoke with Gordon Bethune myself. I tried to make my position crystal clear.

"Gordon," I implored, "we are trying to unite this thing. If you love this company, don't pursue this. Your presence will drive the divide even greater. You have to understand that. And I'm going to fight this to the bitter end, not because of you and not because of anything else but the fact that it's just not the right thing."

I continued to make this argument privately with Brad and Paul. Through a series of conversations in March and into April, I had an opportunity to offer some insights to Brad and Paul about my own experience with proxy battles at CSX in 2008. It was an episode that had become famous as a flash point in the ongoing debate over the wisdom of so-called shareholder activism and a case study in why proxy battles are (usually) a waste of time, money, and energy. It's worth going over some of the details here.

At that time in 2008, in my role as CFO, I was busy attracting investors to our railroad, including giants like Berkshire Hathaway and CAP-RE. They were impressed by CSX's success in strategically improving our operating ratio (in effect, profit margin). Through a series of ambitious initiatives, we were growing earnings and improving costs thanks to the strength of our operational reliability.

Our success also garnered the interest of TCI, a UK-based investment fund known for its "venture philanthropy."

Also called the Children's Investment Fund, it pledged to devote a share of profits to help provide much-needed relief to Africa's starving children. As it happens, one of the principals of the fund during this period was Rishi Sunak, a name you might recognize. He would go on to serve as the UK's Chancellor of the Exchequer, and—as of this writing—occupy Number 10 Downing Street, making history as the first person of color to lead Great Britain as prime minister.

TCI's investment in the railroad proved highly profitable, for them and us, and they lauded our success. Then, things took a turn.

Since performance was so strong, TCI argued to us privately that it would be beneficial to shareholders if CSX jumped into the market and began buying back shares of our stock, boosting its value. To do that, we would have to substantially "lever up" (essentially take on debt).

CSX's management and board considered the idea but eventually rejected it, on the basis that it would detract from our focus on investing in the business and growing the very earnings that TCI wanted to take advantage of in the first place. Not to mention, it risked loading our balance sheet with added debt, which would've been disastrous under any circumstances. And though we didn't know it, the financial crash was just around the corner.

Not deterred by our rejection, TCI informed us that it would go directly to our investors via proxy.

Our team at CSX now had to divert valuable time and resources away from our focus on improving operational efficiency and growing the company. We would have to persuade institutional investors that we had the right strategy in place while TCI's assumptions were flawed. This persuasion campaign would culminate in a vote to determine whose position held merit, our management at CSX or TCI.

To give us a bit of advantage, if only a psychological one, we chose a swampy railyard outside New Orleans as the site for the annual meeting. If the corporate raiders were going to play it tough, so were we. We constructed a large tent in a remote location, setting up operations—it would be our "Alamo," the scene of a fight to the bitter end.

From that tent, I made last-minute calls to every shareholder I could reach, not dissuaded when told it was an inconvenient time. I even got one prominent investor to take my call while he was in the dentist's chair with a mouth full of gauze.

In advance of the vote, TCI and the investment funds had floated the thought that we might want to settle, but we declined. As the time for the vote approached, a Gulf storm opened overhead and nearly swept us away. In the end, it was too little too late. The vote was close, but TCI won several seats on the board.

For all of that Sturm und Drang, TCI attended only a single meeting of the board before selling the shares. It was a tale full of sound and fury that, in the end, signified nothing. No one got what they wanted, and everyone lost something. CSX spent tens of millions that could have more usefully been invested in operations and safety and growing our top-line earnings.

There were many cautionary lessons from that experience that I felt Altimeter and PAR weren't considering.

I explained to Brad and Paul that, given my experience at CSX, they ought to be wary of the unforeseen consequences of moving ahead with a proxy fight. It would be costly and damaging to employee morale. It would paralyze the company just as we were trying to launch a turnaround strategy. And there were no guarantees that it would turn out the way they wanted it to.

At the time, CSX had been strong enough to recover and move on from the 2008 proxy fight with TCI. But United was still so fragile. Surely, we could put the pin back in the grenade, I thought; it wasn't too late for us to avert another drawn-out, expensive, and value-destroying proxy battle. And it wasn't like we were philosophically miles apart, either.

I shared Brad's view that we needed stronger airline experience represented on the board.

The outlines of the deal were within sight, based on the negotiations that our United team and our advisers had orchestrated, prior to the exchange of all those press statements that coincided with the Houston visit. I had already nominated three directors, including two airline experts. Brad and his side had already offered that they were willing to accept only two seats. With more retirements planned that would open more seats, we could agree on who would fill them.

Initially, Brad wanted to be named as a director. I didn't think this was a good idea for a variety of reasons, not least because it wouldn't be good for Brad. If he sat on the board, he would be significantly restricted in his ability to make investments in the industry.

The same thing happened with respect to TCI, I explained to Brad. The victory was a pyrrhic one because once they assumed a role on the board, they found themselves so restricted that they decided the prize they had fought for wasn't worth having in the first place. That's why they vacated their board seat so quickly afterward.

Eventually, both sides agreed that PAR and Altimeter would nominate two board members, with a third that would be mutually agreed upon. I was open to defer assuming the chairmanship so that we could fill it at a later time—just not with Gordon.

They agreed that Gordon would not be nominated and Brad would withdraw his name. As an alternative to Brad, they put forward Ed Shapiro, managing director of PAR. When I met with Ed in my office, I instantly felt that he would make a great addition. He also thoughtfully suggested a few candidates for the third seat, and we shared similar ideas of what we were looking for. This eventual choice would be Ted Phillips, who succeeded me as chairman after my retirement.

By the final week of April, we had reached a settlement. We had successfully averted a proxy battle, and we had strengthened the board in the process. The result had the added effect of blessing the relationship of trust that was growing between labor and management.

As the dust settled, we were finally able to resume the work of building a new United. And I still had more union contracts to finalize.

• • •

Trust is a commodity that resists an easy valuation. But when you need it, it's priceless.

That was true for me during my negotiations with Altimeter and PAR. My union partners stuck their necks out and voiced unequivocal support for me and the direction that I had communicated to their members before my heart attack. They did so even though we still had huge mountains to climb in our negotiations, including for the flight attendants.

Yet they did it all the same.

I hadn't asked Todd Insler or Sara Nelson to make their statements or to organize their members to picket in support of management and me. I couldn't have asked, even if I had thought to do so. The decision to rally their members could only have come from them, and it played an important role in strengthening my hand so we could bring that fraught episode to a conclusion. The result was a stronger board for United and a new narrative about the state of relations between management and labor.

The leaders had trusted me when I promised them that my strategy would put employees first, and that's why they did what they did. This new trust would be tested as contract discussions reached a critical point a few months later. The negotiating teams back at the Palmer House in Chicago had continued to hammer out a deal, fighting hard, pressing for every advantage.

In late summer 2016, I was in Pasadena, California, meeting with investors, when my phone rang very early in the morning.

The caller ID belonged to Sara, and she wasn't happy. Our two teams—the AFA's and United's—were working around the clock in their respective war rooms. She felt our negotiating team was digging in its heels and being unreasonable. The strain was taking a toll on both sides as we worked to close a deal involving hundreds of millions of dollars. I called Mike Bonds, our then human resources chief and head of labor relations, who told me they'd hit a snag. The two parties were still apart on a couple of minor issues that were being highly valued and thus stuck in deliberations.

"Look, Mike," I said. "Let's get this done. Make sure everyone knows that we went the extra distance. But it's time to bring this in for a landing."

I called Sara and asked her to trust me. We would honor the last sticking point in the deal. That was enough for her—as well as for her members who trusted my word because Sara trusted me.

The ultimate deal, which was ratified later in the fall, put the exclamation point to a long and difficult chapter that began in 2010 with the merger. From now on, there would be no distinction between sub-UA employees and the "ex-Cons." This deal laid the groundwork for the last stages of this long courtship to reach its fulfillment, which would happen in September 2018, eight years to the day after the merger began, when the joint agreement between the two work groups was fully concluded. With the final pieces of the puzzle clicking together, the full potential of the new United-Continental could then be fully realized, and our people would finally be allowed to operate on the same aircraft, sharing "common metal." With that, we would finally be flying together.

Sara's team emailed her draft statement about the impending deal. Often, these press release statements are a way for both parties to declare victory over the other, continuing the fight after it's supposed to be finished. The statements also tend to imply more hostility than really exists; after all, it doesn't often help a union boss to be seen as overly chummy with management, or else members might think they didn't fight hard enough on the deal. What she actually wrote touched me. "This contract would not have been possible without the commitment of Oscar Munoz to unite United Airlines," the statement read. I knew those words would echo among my employees.

With contracts in hand and relations with labor soaring and the proxy battle largely resolved, I felt confident about the all-important board meeting that was set for September 2016. This would be the first meeting with new board members, and I knew there may be factionalism to deal with. There was also a new member of the team whom I was proud to introduce to the board, though the news media had been buzzing about the splashy hire for weeks.

"Investors decided Tuesday that adding Scott Kirby to the United Airlines turnaround formula made the company worth $1.5 billion more," reported *Fortune* in August 2016.

Hiring Scott Kirby, president of our rival American Airlines, a US Air Force veteran, and one of the biggest names—and personalities—in our business, marked a major coup that rocked the industry. After a decade as president of American Airlines, Scott had expected to take over as CEO of the Dallas-based airline. When that didn't happen, Scott became a free agent. I didn't want someone with Scott's combined streaks of intelligence and competitiveness to be playing against me.

Fortunately, Ed Shapiro—who had been the consensus candidate from PAR Capital, helping to avert the proxy battle—had brokered a connection with Scott. Ed's reputation, fortified by a stellar track record of investing in the airline industry, made him the ideal person to build this bridge, though I was careful not to step over lines of legality as well as courtesy toward our colleagues in Dallas.

No promises about a potential future for Scott at United were given and none asked for. But in getting to know him, I could see that this was someone who understood what I was trying to accomplish and, in fact, he was surprised to see United's leadership finally willing to think outside of its traditional playbook.

By bringing Scott on board and offering him the president role, I knew I was essentially signaling that he would be my successor. Most leaders have a sword of Damocles hanging over their heads, reminding them that their time is finite. The wisest leaders begin to develop their successors early on, which provides the next CEO time to gain experience, establish themselves, and signal that the company will remain on a steady course after a potential transition.

Yet I was less than a year into a job and there remained a question mark over my health.

Was I prepared to start the countdown clock this early in my tenure? Would it, in fact, precipitate my premature departure? Was I confident that Scott would support my employee-focused turnaround philosophy? Obviously, I would step down eventually, likely after a five-year term. When that happened, did I have confidence that he was the right person to carry the employee-first agenda forward?

Scott and I are vastly different people, with different personalities and styles. United and American are also long-standing rivals, sharing several key hubs where we fight like hell for market share.

His reputation as the best airline strategist in the business was uncontested, and his experience supplemented mine. Likewise, his in-your-face personality and direct style contrasted with but complemented my own.

However, I knew he had often rubbed people in the industry the wrong way, giving off an indication that he cared only about the numbers and not the people. Yet once I got to know Scott better, I quickly came to understand that he was precisely the person who could develop our strategy. Yes, he showed an aggressive need to win. But that is a quality you want in a number two. I remember my days as president and chief operating officer of CSX. I was well known for my no-holds-barred attitude toward boosting profits and maximizing efficiencies. That's what my boss, Michael Ward, expected of me. When I transitioned to the top job at United, I understood that my new role was different, requiring that I demonstrate different qualities. The same skills that made me an effective number two at CSX would not translate to what United needed from its CEO.

I could tell that Scott possessed that ability to grow and develop in a similar way, especially if given a runway of several years. In the meantime, I needed a fighter, and that's what Scott is. Moreover, we would need his industry-wide credibility to sell skeptical board members and investors on the bold strategic moves we were beginning to contemplate.

When we announced that Scott would be leaving American Airlines to join its archrival United, Gordon Bethune magnanimously praised the move, to his great credit. He also recognized how difficult it is to give up a part of one's own title to bring someone on board who may one day succeed you. I appreciated his kind words.

Scott and I would have to walk in lockstep if we were going to capitalize on our improved relations with labor and devise a new phase of our business strategy that would cement United's turnaround.

Having competed against United, Scott understood the strength of our hub-and-spoke structure, which was the envy of the industry. He told me he had spent years imagining how he would unlock the potential of that route network if ever given the chance, something United had thus far failed to achieve. Once he had an opportunity to really take a look under the hood, his diagnosis was pure Scott: "You've been playing defense when you should have been playing offense."

Throughout 2017, we would get to work devising this new game plan that would finally deliver United to profitability. This would require cooperation between the heads of various functions—network planning, revenue management, as well as the chief financial officer—and they each had strong, often conflicting viewpoints.

To help me wrangle these competing power centers and get them to work together, I needed to hire a new chief of staff to replace Kate, whom I had promoted by this point to a bigger role. Mandeep Grewal was the perfect choice. Her background across the company and her fluent knowledge of revenue management gave her excellent relationships to shepherd this complicated process.

A veteran of both Continental and United, Mandeep possessed an innate understanding for how I could best communicate across both legacy halves of the company and across many cultures. Raised in both New Delhi, India, and Zambia, Africa, Mandeep pursued an aviation career, following in her mother's footsteps, who broke one of the highest and hardest glass ceilings as one of India's first female aviators. With so many crises unfolding at once, I was glad to have her advising me during this critical period, someone so knowledgeable of the company and with jet fuel running in her veins.

Sonja had also taken a leap in her career, taking new jobs throughout the company, and when I elevated Kate to the C-Suite, Sonja would join her team. To succeed Sonja, I drafted an experienced executive assistant, Jamie Smith, who would become a de facto deputy chief of staff. Hailing from McKinsey, the consultancy firm, Jamie was baptized by fire during these events and never missed a beat. With an uncanny ability to see around corners and an unflappable demeanor, she knew how to lighten the mood when situations became decidedly dark. Raised in a Notre Dame family, she would set a miniature Notre Dame golden football helmet on her desk, placed exactly so I'd see it whenever I walked out of my office—precisely to get a rise out of me, being a USC alum. When she stepped away, I'd hide that helmet, only to find it again sitting on my own desk when I returned later.

We would eventually call a truce, agreeing that I would attend her parents' famous annual tailgate at the Notre Dame game, but she would also pay a visit to our USC tent.

Soon, I would need that camaraderie more than ever, because we were heading into some rough air.

CHAPTER 15

ROUGH AIR

On Saturday, April 8, 2017, sixteen months after my transplant surgery, I chaired the Chicago Heart Ball, the American Heart Association's premier fundraising event. My heart attack and heart transplant had captured the city's attention, and this was my chance to return the love and support I'd benefited from during those difficult months.

It promised to be a wonderful evening. Chicago's famous winds had calmed, and the temperature rose nearly to shirtsleeves weather, balmy for that time of year. I felt in great health, and United was back on course. As the sun began to set, guests in black ties and evening dresses began to arrive at Chicago's Festival Hall, which sits at the terminus of Navy Pier, stretching deep into the harbor and surrounded by the waters of Lake Michigan.

I stepped onstage and shook hands with the mayor. In that inimitable style of big-city ward politics, Rahm pulled me in and gave me a quick verbal barb. "I thought I was the one to give you that heart attack, Oscar," he joked, remembering our meeting at City Hall the day before it happened.

I looked out on a sea of red, with hundreds of dinner tables stretching across the hall, draped in scarlet linen and festooned with red and white roses.

Happily, former board chairman Henry Meyer had made the effort to fly to Chicago to be with us. As did John Walker, who had been one of the directors who magnanimously agreed to step down to make room for the picks made by the activist investors. His presence in support of me that evening demonstrated his friendship and largeness of character. I was indebted to them for sticking with me and keeping the faith during those dark days.

But the true VIPs—at least in my eyes—were the invited guests who'd played a role in my survival and sat at the head tables: Cathy and the kids, as well as Mandeep and Jamie; the two EMTs who rescued me that morning as I lay bleeding on the floor of my apartment. My doctors from Northwestern Memorial Hospital, including Flaherty, Pham, and Anderson, especially enjoyed regaling their tablemates with details of my survival. I had also invited a group of United flight attendants who had responded to cardiac events in midair and saved lives.

"The experience of being on the heart transplant wait list is one of those great equalizers," I told the audience. "You can't buy your way to the top. You can't predict when you might be called, or if you ever will. The experience is also a great uniter among those who go through it."

As I spoke, I locked eyes with one person. "There isn't a single family that hasn't been touched by heart disease," I said, "including my United family. When I was laying in the hospital waiting for a transplant, I met a fellow heart patient—and a United flight attendant—named Fernando Falcone."

"We became close," I said, tears welling in my eyes. "I've invited him to be my guest of honor because he is now waiting for that same miracle call that I received on my birthday, and a heart transplant."

As I said this, the entire audience looked to Fernando. The last time I had seen him, we both were in medical gowns. Now, we were dressed in tuxedos, though he was still hooked to an LVAD. I could feel the scars itching underneath my clothing, where my LVAD had once been implanted.

As the audience rose to their feet to applaud him, I saw his devoted partner sitting beside him, beaming with pride. But I knew the stress they both were under as they waited for him to receive a compatible heart.

Though I didn't know it, this would be the last time I would ever see Fernando; he passed away while still on the transplant list.

I've said before that the bonds of "La Familia" are not exclusively ones of blood relations but are born of common experience. As Fernando looked back at me, speechless, as the applause continued, I felt I had gained yet one more brother in my life, and his eventual passing only increased my own sense of indebtedness and responsibility to be worthy of the second chance that I'd been randomly granted.

· · ·

As the 2017 Heart Ball wound to a close, we had successfully raised the most money in the event's history. Cathy and the kids were exhausted and the six of us realized the night had kept us so busy that most of us had barely eaten. My son Kevin called ahead for a feast of Domino's pizza to be delivered to our apartment. Though Cathy and I had originally thought we would move to Chicago full-time and purchase a house big enough for the whole family in the suburbs, we had decided to put that plan on permanent hold. After all, we didn't know whether I would remain on the transplant list in Tampa or not; and, in fact, we didn't even know if I would survive in my United job at all. Though Cathy and I were dealing as best we could with the glare that attended my job and the guesswork of my heart situation, at the end of the day we were just parents wanting the best for our kids, as any parent would. Our youngest son, Jack, had only just begun high school and was thriving—establishing a devoted circle of friends, excelling in class, playing on the football and lacrosse teams, growing into a more thoughtful and mature young man with every day. As parents, we couldn't disrupt all of that for the sake of my job, and we felt he deserved to enjoy the same typical and carefree teenage experience that his siblings had.

But that meant Cathy would need to remain most of the time in Florida with Jack, with the responsibilities that rightfully belong to two parents often falling on her own two shoulders. This was the first time Cathy,

Jack, and I had ever been separated in any meaningful way, for any length of time, and while I tried to get back home to them as often as I could, I knew I was missing the milestones in Jack's life that I hadn't missed for his brothers and sisters—to see him out there playing under the lights of a Friday-night game, homecoming dances, and the million moments of adolescence that never come around again. Yet as I spent many days far away from them, trying to keep the United family together, Cathy—ever displaying the grace and so many other gifts that drew me to her in the very first place—kept our little family together and on track in my absence.

Finally, on this night, we were back together, all six of us, and we didn't want to share the moment with a ballroom full of people.

So we decided to head home early while the party continued without us. A blast of cool air greeted us as we burst out of the brilliantly lit ballroom of Navy Pier and into the Chicago evening, still basking in the happy glow of the party and the joy of finally being together as a family.

I felt like pinching myself in case this was a flashback to one of those post-op, painkiller-induced hallucinations I'd briefly experienced, half suspecting that I would awake to find myself back in the hospital room. I was carrying a vintage electric guitar that was given to me that night by the AHA, which had belonged to my favorite band, the Rolling Stones. I thought of the song that was playing in the background as they wheeled me into the operating room for the transplant, "You Can't Always Get What You Want."

To be blessed with such unearned fortune as a husband and father, to be the recipient of so much generosity and support as a heart transplant survivor, to have my family gather all in one place, for us all to be in health and happiness . . . well, the moment felt dreamlike. This is precisely what Cathy and I had hoped and prayed might happen. We didn't dare believe it might come true, that—indeed—we might get what we wanted, this time.

I knew it was the perfect conclusion and coda to the nightmare of my heart drama, the end of a long and painful chapter in our lives. Our family walked arm in arm, smiling from ear to ear, down the boardwalk to our car. The city lights ranged along the shoreline ahead of us, and the starlight of a cold, cloudless night shone above us with razor-sharp clarity. Lake Michigan was still thawing. Most of it was still frozen into sheets of ice, as if the waves had been stopped in time. I would soon wish time had really frozen in that moment. I would've cherished the chance to pause, to remember every detail, to hold on to it for a little while longer.

• • •

Back in the family apartment, we stayed up late laughing and telling stories. Sunday morning was quiet, and that afternoon I began to prepare for the week ahead. Early that evening my phone rang.

It was Todd Insler, head of the pilots' union. "Oscar, have you seen this?"

He described an incident that happened only an hour or so earlier at Chicago O'Hare Airport on United flight 3411 bound for Louisville, Kentucky, operated by our partners at United Express. The flight, scheduled for takeoff at 5:40 p.m., was sold out.

The logistical dance of airline operations is like a monumental, globally scaled game of musical chairs, one in which—ideally—the game keeps going but without anyone having to lose their chair. A single problem in any part of the system can cause a chain reaction of bad things happening.

On that Sunday afternoon, with a packed regional plane full of people who were probably tired and frustrated, just wanting to get home from the weekend, the music stopped. And there weren't enough chairs to go around. Everything that could go wrong went as wrong as it possibly could.

Here's what happened.

A crew was needed in Louisville for a flight operated by our regional partner airline, Express Jet, that was scheduled to take off the following morning. If no crew was in place, that flight would be delayed by hours until another crew could be flown there, somehow. The problem: the crew needed in Louisville was stuck in Chicago. There was only one flight left, 3411.

It then fell to gate agents to persuade ticketed passengers to accept later flights and financial incentives to take other flights. When not enough passengers volunteered, gate agents did what procedures told them to do—using a computer-generated algorithm that automatically selected passengers to rebook. There was no way they could have known which passengers were selected. One of them was Dr. David Dao, who refused all offers. By 7:30 that evening, smartphone videos documented a violent incident showing airport law enforcement wrestling Dr. Dao out of his seat into the aisle and then dragging him off the plane, his glasses knocked from his eyes to below his nose, blood gushing from his face. Videos from different perspectives began to generate massive numbers of views on social media, and soon those videos were being played almost constantly on cable news. Viewers could hear the doctor's screams followed by distressed cries from fellow passengers.

It was wrong. It was shameful. It was avoidable. Now, it was a crisis.

Monday morning was our regularly scheduled E-Team meeting. The key decision-makers would be there, and I asked that our corporate communications chief join us to discuss the latest situation and how we should address it.

Immediately after the incident on flight 3411, the United Twitter account featured brief statements designed to seek more information and to assure customers that "we prioritize the safety of each individual." Unfortunately, our next tweet at 6:00 a.m. Monday threw gas on the fire. We stated that the flight had been "overbooked." This turned out not even to be true; the flight was, in fact, never overbooked—just sold out.

We then used Twitter to apologize for miscommunicating the initial facts of the situation. This statement only made us look like we were quibbling about details. The Twittersphere roared to life with thousands of complaints and insults: customers outraged at United for poor customer service, cramped flights, and all the bad food they'd experienced on every commercial airline for their entire lives. We deserved their outrage for this incident, but it had also become the focal point for decades of unhappiness.

At around 10:00 a.m., still in the heat of the moment, I stepped out of the E-Team meeting to work on a new statement, one that was intended to come from me:

"This is an upsetting event to all of us here at United. I apologize for having to reaccommodate these customers. Our team is moving with a sense of urgency to work with the authorities and conduct our own detailed review of what happened. We are also reaching out to this passenger to talk directly to him and further address and resolve this situation."

On top of the initial mistake of framing the issue as an overbooking situation, now we'd touched a new nerve by replacing the word "overbooked' with "reaccommodate." The word was cold and clinical, cringe-inducing in its inappropriateness to the horror that was playing across every screen in the world. My poor choice of words was something reminiscent of Orwellian doublespeak, words that fly in the face of what you can see plainly with your own eyes. And, to think, only a few months earlier I had been named *PR* magazine's "Communicator of the Year."

Anyone who watched the video knew the passenger was not "reaccommodated." He was bloodied and dragged off the airplane. Impossible as it is to believe, at this point only a few people sitting around the E-Team table had even seen the video, other than myself. PR malpractice doesn't begin to explain it, and I daily berate myself for letting it happen.

The first thing our head of corporate communications and I should have done, before we issued any statement at all, was to demand that the entire executive team watch the video together. I should have forced us to watch it over and over again until we couldn't stand it, and then watch it ten more times until any inclination that we could minimize the damage with a sterile apology was out the window.

But I didn't do that. Already a crisis, the incident was now spiraling out of control. This is when the loneliness of the CEO becomes most acute. Even your closest colleagues are beginning to back away from you. And it is during these times that you can't let that happen. You need to be open, listen, and seek counsel from a variety of perspectives.

By evening, I had sent a letter to all employees acknowledging our mistakes. I also wanted them to know that I emphatically stood behind them, and that together we would go above and beyond to ensure we fly right. At the same time, an incident report—a summary that is generated whenever a significant event takes place with a passenger—was released. Its robotic language, as well as words like "belligerent" that seemed to assign blame to Dr. Dao, released another firestorm, and we were back to square one.

I got on a flight that evening to Washington, DC, where airline executives were gathering for a regularly scheduled meeting. I reviewed the day's events and prepared for the next day's discussions, but after landing I was advised to stay out of the public eye. The temperature had continued to rise, and it was likely that TV crews would be looking for me to make another statement.

Tuesday morning, after conversations with board members and executive staff, I asked that we widen our circle of advisers. Chief among them was Richard Edelman, whose Trust Barometer has become an influential checkpoint for consumer brands. Coverage of the fiasco had become the dominant news story on every channel, in every social media platform.

The incident report was now scorching through social media and we were beginning to receive reports of harassment, verbal and otherwise, of our employees, both on the job and in their daily lives. Employees were getting heat from family members and friends, offering their own apologies in place of the ones I had failed to get right so far. I knew I would have only one last opportunity to explain myself if I was going to begin to bring the temperature down.

No one could write this one for me. It had to come from the heart, even if—especially if—it would be the last thing I did as CEO.

"The truly horrific event that occurred on this flight has elicited many responses from all of us: outrage, anger, disappointment," I wrote. "I share all of those sentiments, and one above all: my deepest apologies for what happened."

I know that if Brett Hart, our legal counsel and my closest confidant, had been present on that first day, this would have been the first statement we made. By revealing my personal anguish at what I saw in that video, there was an opportunity—albeit a small one—that people would be willing to listen, understand, and forgive.

"Oscar, you need to go on TV," the Edelman team advised.

They were right. There is a moment when the entire enterprise, the character of the company and its people, relies on a single person, the CEO.

I had made it my mission to break down the barriers between management and the company, to bond myself with those I led. Now, I had gotten my wish. A global audience was about to watch me, and they would make no distinction between United and myself.

We decided that the next morning I would appear on *Good Morning America* to answer for myself and for United Airlines. From then on, I listened to well-meaning advice, and I prepped for my appearance by revisiting the tool kit of tried-and-true media tactics that leaders use to avoid saying the wrong thing: What are the three messages you must air? If the question is this, then what is your answer? What is your sound-bite message? If cornered, how will you pivot?

By the time I landed in Chicago and returned home, I was upside down, with advice coming from every angle, most of it conflicting. I was still unsure what I'd say early the next morning when the cameras started rolling.

It was late, and I needed to get some sleep. I lay in bed, the competing messages and words of advice I'd been given still spinning in my head. Around two or three in the morning I sat upright—the gravity of my challenge and what was at stake for United lodged in my gut.

The next thing I knew, I had dropped to my knees. I'm not a pious person, but it was that kind of moment. Kneeling there beside the bed, I thought of Mama Josefina, who had always been my most formative role model. I thought about my heritage, my duties to my family, and my debt to my United family. I was searching for guidance and direction. I'm not going to say it was an answered prayer, but it came to me very clearly: Tell the truth as best you know it. Be accountable. Blaming others would have been anathema to my grandmother. I never heard her complain about a single thing in her life. There was only one thing to say that mattered and reflected how I felt as a human being: I'm sorry and I will fix it.

I never went back to sleep, but I lay down again and felt a calmness I'd not felt before. I didn't know the exact words I'd use when I sat down with ABC News in a few hours, but I knew it would come from my heart. I would take ownership for our mistakes. I would be honest. I had no other choice, really, because I also knew that whatever I said, I was going to be asked about it for the rest of my life. So I better get it right.

By the time I sat down in the chair, I had a firm idea of what I needed to communicate: "We let policies and procedures get ahead of doing what's right."

After reminding me that there had been calls to boycott United, Rebecca Jarvis, ABC's chief business and economics correspondent, led off with what everyone wanted to know.

"What did you think when you watched that video?"

"It's not so much what I thought, it's what I felt," I replied. "The word 'shame' comes to mind. I want to apologize to Dr. Dao, to his family and the passengers on that flight." My response was so immediate, it jolted even me. I'm sure if the studio lights hadn't obscured my vision, I would've seen the communications gurus and legal folks gnashing their teeth. So much for media training.

"I want to apologize to our customers and employees," I continued. "That is not who our family at United is. You saw us at a bad moment. This can never happen again on a United Airlines flight. That's my premise and that's my promise."

Jarvis wasn't quite ready to let me off the hook. She pressed on: "Why not communicate that in your early statements—you talked about reaccommodate and you talked about a disruptive and belligerent passenger. Why did it take until Tuesday to offer a more fullhearted apology?"

I answered that we needed to get the facts. But I acknowledged that my words fell short, and that I'd learned from that.

What will you do?

We will review the policies that led to this. The use of law enforcement aboard an aircraft has to be looked at closely.

What went wrong?

It was a system failure. We had not provided our frontline supervisors and managers with the proper tools and procedures to use common sense. They have common sense. That's on me.

What needs to change?

When you are boarded, seated, and situated, we need to empower the frontline staff with expanded policies that allow more common sense. A law enforcement official will never remove a booked, seated passenger.

Is Dr. Dao at fault in any way?

No. He can't be. No one should be treated that way, period.

A lot of PR professionals have said this was awful and have called for your resignation. Have you considered resigning?

No. I was hired to make United better, and we've been doing that and that's what we will continue to do.

The interview ended and I thanked Ms. Jarvis. I walked the several blocks back to the Willis Tower. There is something incredibly odd about being watched on television by millions of people, then walking anonymously down the street as if it's a normal day.

When I reached the office, my first stop was a visit to our corporate communications team. The members of this small group had essentially nothing to do with the several communications mistakes that led us to this point. Yet they had been receiving the brunt of the onslaught.

I wanted to shake the hands of these younger people who had joined the company at a time of hope and optimism, and yet had spent a series of all-nighters fielding calls from incandescent reporters and angry customers, even receiving death threats.

My next step was to apologize to United customers:

[This] happened because our corporate policies were placed ahead of our shared values. Our procedures got in the way of our employees doing what they know is right.

Fixing that problem starts now with changing how we fly, serve, and respect our customers. This is a turning point for all of us here at United—and as CEO, it's my responsibility to make sure that we learn from this experience and redouble our efforts to put our customers at the center of everything we do.

I believe we must go further in redefining what United's corporate citizenship looks like in our society. You can and ought to expect more from us, and we intend to live up to those higher expectations in the way we embody social responsibility and civic leadership everywhere we operate. I hope you will see that pledge express itself in our actions going forward, of which these initial, though important, changes are merely a first step.

Our goal should be nothing less than to make you truly proud to say, "I fly United."

With United's reputation still in a nosedive, these lofty words may have seemed risible. My team cautioned against widening the aperture of the letter's focus and linking this incident to a broader social mission. But I believed that so many of our missteps over the course of the crisis resulted from our inclination to minimize the issue, to run away from responsibility, when in fact what we should have done was demonstrate what George Orwell described as "The Power of Facing."

The public rage incited by flight 3411 was primarily about the horrendous incident itself, but it also tapped into broader feelings of social alienation, of people not taking time to recognize and respect one another, and a sense that big companies simply don't care about the individual person.

United had not created this broad social phenomenon of distrust between customer and company, but we had an opportunity to take a lead in addressing it. In fact, the horrendousness of what had occurred accelerated our efforts to completely reimagine our culture of caring for the customer and one another. If there was anyone left in the company who had yet to "get religion" on our turnaround vision, the flight 3411 incident made zealous converts of them.

As promised, we returned at the end of April with a series of concrete fixes to prevent this from happening again, including increasing incentives for voluntary rebooking up to $10,000. We also eliminated the red tape on permanently lost bags with a new "no-questions-asked" $1,500 reimbursement policy.

Yet the question remained of how to ensure safety and security while allowing enough freedom to employees for them to exercise their own judgment in the moment. In a post–9/11 world, I don't think anyone wants to have a fast and loose operational culture in the skies.

Too few rules and things can go just as badly as 3411, or much worse.

Kate Gebo had recently been promoted to become executive vice president for human resources. She, along with then chief customer officer Toby Enqvist, spearheaded a company-wide mission and developed a new approach to customer caring and employee training that would solve that puzzle. After rigorous work, we unveiled our "core4 principles." Safe. Caring. Dependable. Efficient.

We invested tens of millions of dollars in new, innovative training techniques. We continuously reinforced the message with all our employees: We trust you to make the right choice. You know what it means to care for your customer, and you know how to balance that caring with keeping us efficient. If it comes down to helping a customer in need, even if that means allowing a small delay in departure, that's your prerogative.

It didn't happen overnight, with plenty of skeptics doubting that we meant what we said. But eventually our employees rediscovered their own sense of self-confidence. Increasingly, they didn't have a supervisor glaring over their shoulder. They found they were receiving more customers saying "Thank you" and having to say "I'm sorry" less often.

• • •

This flexible approach proved effective, and in later years Toby's team would scale it up into a new training model we called "Backstage."

We built out a large, beautifully designed event space where members of in-flight crews participated in interactive workshops that updated them on the latest training and skills to help better serve our customers and each other in the sky. In addition to training, the event served as a well-deserved celebration, with flight attendants being treated the way we would want them to treat our customers—like VIPs. There was music and dancing, top-flight food and drinks. It was a celebration, but also a demonstration—of "proof, not promise"—that we valued the contributions they made. We put them up in the historic Palmer Hotel, which was somewhat ironic as it was the same hotel where union negotiations took place.

Frontline employees had often complained to me that they never got any "face time" with the leaders of the company. Over the span of thirty-five weeks, our senior officers and I made ourselves available for hours on end at Backstage events. A line of employees would zigzag for hundreds of feet, all queuing up to look me in the eye and tell me everything that they had felt for so long. Some of the comments were encouraging, others were harsh, but I never left until almost every single person who wanted to talk to me had their opportunity.

The investment in core4 and Backstage paid off.

These principles—firm but allowing the flexibility for employees to use their own judgment—would become crucial during the pandemic that would come years later, when we had to pare down our service in so many ways to keep us COVID-safe. We knew that the stresses made flying a truly difficult experience during those dark months. Yet even with the COVID restrictions, our employees felt they had the structure and support to solve problems at their discretion, to de-escalate and put passengers first, even at risk to their own health.

In a sad hour in our history, when kindness and appreciation in the skies seem to never have been in shorter supply, our employees delivered a surfeit of service that brings healing and hope.

• • •

The lessons derived from a careful analysis of the 3411 crisis, its causes, our response, and the lasting effects are ones that all companies would benefit from—not merely in the airline industry but in all industries, and not only for CEOs and leaders in the corporate sector but leaders of any organization.

Not a day goes by that I don't think about what occurred on flight 3411. Instead of avoiding the issue, I choose to keep it top of mind. Rather than running from it, I often remind people of it. That's because it illustrates what can happen when employees are hamstrung by policies and procedures rather than empowered to exercise their own judgment and set of sturdy values, and also when a leader pays heed to legalistic caution rather than their better angels.

I continue to ask myself hard questions. What good were all those early efforts at damage control when the damage had been done even before law enforcement had stepped onto that plane, before this person had purchased a ticket, before the first photo was snapped or video posted?

It started when United employees were put in an impossible position, forced to choose between doing the right thing—the human, common-sense thing—and their job security if they didn't follow the rigid protocols. It started with a company that had drilled procedures rather than values into our culture, rewarding metrics and not meaningful interactions. It started with the people in charge. Although what occurred on that aircraft was the result of select individuals exceeding any limits of what constitutes acceptable law enforcement and did not directly involve any airline employees, especially any United Airlines employees, ultimately the blame for what happened and the results that followed belonged with one person only: me.

The most basic test of a leader is the strength of their commitment to what is true. The truth was that I felt as much outrage as anyone when I saw that viral video of a fellow human being in pain and mistreated at the hands of law enforcement on our aircraft.

And yet I wasn't honest about it; and once people can tell you aren't being honest in the first instance, they won't listen to anything else you say—and rightly so.

The initial statements that seemed so clinical and hollow deserved the outrage and disbelief they received.

At a more fundamental level, I didn't demand that the people around me be honest about what they'd witnessed on that video, how they felt about our part in it, and their feelings of betrayal, guilt, and fear.

As difficult as it is to delve so deeply into something that is so painful to recall, there is no honest way to tell the story of United's turnaround without it. In fact, I would go further and say there is no way to understand how United has become the airline and company it is today, how it survived the pandemic, without understanding this crucible moment. It served as the inflection point and remains the touchstone by which we test and measure the quality of all our efforts.

. . .

The year 2017 didn't get much easier from there—from pets that passed away on our aircraft to a host of increasingly exotic emotional support animals being denied boarding, including a full-grown peacock. In the middle of the 3411 crisis, a scorpion literally fell from the overhead compartment onto a passenger—fortunately no one was hurt.

Next, we hosted a third quarter earnings call that will go down as one of the most disastrous in recent memory.

Wall Street investors had already become wary of the strategic moves we'd begun to make that telegraphed the growth plan we'd been developing. Our various teams hadn't yet coalesced behind the details of the strategy, and the analysts on the call could tell. Our responses were muddled and inconsistent, sparking concerns that we were poised to grow irresponsibly, without a fixed plan, which would negatively reverberate industry-wide.

Many of our investors owned shares in competitor airlines and they didn't want to hear about our growth plans.

By the end of the day our stock fell 12 percent, the largest single-day drop for UAL in six years. Demands for my firing escalated from shouts to shrieks.

Though an inauspicious beginning, that extreme low point in my tenure marked the moment when, as a United team, we decided to pick ourselves off the ground, dust ourselves off, and finally start playing to win.

We had been on a losing streak, but we were getting close to unveiling for investors the full extent of our plan to drive sustainably higher profits and margins.

We owed everyone a winning streak for United: to our employees, and to everyone who depended on us to be a great airline once again; to every individual shareholder who had invested their hard-earned money or had their retirement savings tied into pension funds that depended on our profitability. We owed it to every small business owner who operated in a small city or community and relied on their local airline to work for them, so they could connect to markets and grow their businesses. Personally, I felt I owed it to everyone who had kept faith with me, through cardiac arrest and PR crises, believing that I could ultimately deliver for them.

Finally, we owed it to everyone who had sacrificed something during the painful integration between Continental and United, believing in my promises that better days lay ahead on the other side.

CHAPTER 16

NEW FLIGHT PLAN

United was a sleeping giant. The merger had knitted together a global route network with the greatest potential for profitability in the industry, which would serve customers and investors well. But we had not realized that potential, partly because we were afraid of precisely the type of negative reaction that we received on that third quarter earnings call.

The investment community believed that the only path to profitability for a legacy airline like United was to shrink and cede competitive markets to low-cost carriers. And for a decade, that's exactly what we did, retreating from competitive markets. Investors feared that growing would make us go bust while triggering a price war that might hurt the entire industry. It was a grave mistake, and as the saying goes, "When your enemies are making mistakes, don't interrupt them." Our competitors weren't interrupting us as we continued to dig a hole for ourselves, deeper and deeper.

One might ask, Why is it so important to appease Wall Street? Shouldn't an airline focus more on giving customers what they want?

The answer is that an airline has many stakeholders, and our business is capital intensive (airplanes aren't cheap to buy). That means we need to ensure we can raise capital from the equity and debt markets, in both the short and the long term, to survive.

We must manage our business to meet the demands of every stake-holder, sure, but it is a straightforward fact that investors hold an ownership stake in the company. It is our job to generate value for them and increase the value of the company. We owed them a detailed plan and we were going to sit in the penalty box until we rolled that out the following January.

One might also ask, Why would growth be looked upon skeptically by these investors?

It seems like a simple concept: if you want to grow your business, you must provide a consistent and reliable service that customers want and on which they can depend. In a capital-intensive business, you also need to show a reliable pattern of earning a return above your cost of capital. United as well as our peer airlines had a choppy record ... and into this we were doubling down on growth.

With twenty-twenty hindsight it's very clear that we were right. But at the time it was foolish to expect enthusiasm from risk-shy investors in the historically cyclical airline sector.

And we knew that the growth strategy we were developing bucked the conventional philosophy of airline management. To understand how that's so, let me give you a short primer on how airlines actually make money.

Let's start with the traditional playbook.

Each legacy carrier has focused historically on tightly managing capacity (the total seats an airline offers) to maximize pricing and yields and thus maintain profit margins. But ultimately you have to grow the top line (and do so profitably) if you want to create shareholder value.

On top of that, the legacy airline business is about connectivity. A hub's connectivity grows exponentially as you add incremental flights. Think about it. If you have fifty flights all departing at the same time during the day (what we call a "single bank") and you add one more flight in the mix, then you've just added fifty more connection opportunities.

It's called growth, and American Airlines and Delta Airlines had managed to grow while United shrank. We needed to catch up and move ahead.

In theory, growth and profit margins should not be mutually exclusive. If you can operate an efficient network with on-time service and reliability to customers, the resulting lower cost structure should therefore enable profitable market share gains. With that in mind, "Just how tight are the profit margins for airlines?"

The consulting firm Oliver Wyman came up with a calculation to answer that question. Its metric: How much of the total revenue earned from a single hundred-passenger flight does an individual passenger account for?

On that hypothetical flight, twenty-nine passengers would pay just for the price of the gas for the trip. The next twenty passengers would pay salaries and employee benefits. By far, the two biggest expenses for any airline are fuel and labor, especially for a union-based airline. Next, the ticket price of sixteen passengers would pay for the ownership costs of the aircraft itself as well as insurance for accident and liability. Fourteen passenger tickets would cover the collective federal taxes, eleven the maintenance costs, and nine passengers would cover the miscellaneous costs, such as in-flight food and beverage, as well as ancillary costs like the rent at the airport and legal fees.

Portions of passengers would pay for the landing fees that grant the airplane use of airport runways and taxiways. Finally, out of all one hundred passengers on the flight, the last passenger would represent pure profit for the airline.

The big takeaway: a single passenger determines whether that flight makes money or loses money.

That slender margin means that every single seat needs to be filled and every plane booked to the maximum for the airline to remain profitable. Any extra capacity in the system needs to be eliminated or it will drag the entire revenue model into the red and therefore compromise the ability of the airline to generate free cash flow and reinvest in the business.

(As I write this, profitability for United is on a very strong trajectory and very likely to expand profit margins, such that as many as ten to fifteen of the passengers on an average flight represent profitability. This is due in large part to the connectivity that our growth plan enabled.)

Making a flight profitable within these tight constraints means solving a very basic math problem.

For people who enjoy solving puzzles, there is simply nothing more fascinating than the airline business, though it requires mastering some very steep gatekeeper language, like CASM, RASM, and PRASM, load factors and yields, concepts that resist the commonsense notions of "supply and demand" that most consumers deal with in their daily lives.

Let me explain. A given airplane will fly a certain number of seats over a total number of miles. Multiply those two numbers together and you get the available seat mile (ASM), or the amount of capacity a flight can generate. So 500 available seats on a plane that flies 1,000 miles have just flown 500,000 "seat miles." In 2019, a typical pre-pandemic year, United flew about 285 billion ASMs.

The cost of operating one seat for one mile flown represents the cost per available seat mile (CASM). The financial success of an airline is determined by how much total revenue it generates per seat, per mile, or the revenue per available seat mile (RASM) to cover the cost of flying that seat per mile.

Except . . . more flying to more destinations implies greater operating costs in the short term as well as more capacity in the market, and more capacity typically means less pricing power. This is why investors punish airlines for growth.

Fewer flights means stronger yields and a maximization of the profit per seat sold and mile flown—hence, the conventional wisdom that prevailed among cautious investors and why they were scared that network growth would lead to a price war between airlines, thus smaller profit margins.

This is the catch-22 that had tangled up United. In order to realize the full potential of our route network, we would need to increase flying (increase ASMs). Investors didn't have confidence that we could increase flying and keep our costs low and, most important, keep our revenue high.

Old United's solution to this Gordian knot was to cut capacity across the system, which would reduce operating costs—since we were flying less—and ensure a higher RASM. Of course, the flip side is this: less flying means fewer tickets, therefore less total revenue, yet higher unit costs.

As I've explained, under the previous leadership, United had promised Wall Street that the airline would deliver $1 billion in savings over several years. The relentless staff shrinkages and cost-cutting measures that led United to sell its landing slots at JFK were the result. We were also flying small fifty-seat aircraft, operated by regional partners, on routes that should be serviced by large customer-friendly aircraft operated by our mainline service.

United would make less money, but it would make sure RASM stayed high. Managing to revenue, not to margin: this was a disastrous strategy that eventually would lead to United losing relevance.

To be fair, some of this strategy was born out of the fact that most of the senior leadership, post-merger, came from Continental, which was a smaller airline than the old United, operating major hubs in Houston and Newark and a much smaller one in Cleveland (which would later be shut down). Transitioning from just three hubs to seven, post-merger, required a different playbook than the one it had become comfortable using.

I learned from my days growing our network and top-line trajectory at CSX that you can't run a huge network, especially one as large as United's, by trying to cut and hope to keep costs low. You have to utilize the unused slack that's been left and start flying more often, to more places that people want to travel, and invest in delivering a product that people want to buy.

The introduction of budget airlines and ultra-low-cost carriers only made the old Continental model even more obsolete. Greater competition on price between high-demand routes like Los Angeles to Denver, for example, requires an airline like United to segment our product to compete against all types of carriers. This is where the introduction of offerings like "Basic Economy" comes in.

On the other hand, smaller routes like Springfield, Illinois, to Chicago are where United thrives, and that's for three reasons.

First, United is probably the only airline that is able to offer such a unique route.

Second, with the right size aircraft we can be sure to fill each flight.

Third, a customer originating from Springfield can connect through a hub like Chicago and continue their journey on a second United flight to hundreds of destinations.

In other words, by not expanding our routes into these secondary markets, we were leaving money on the table—and leaving customers out in the cold—when we should have been capitalizing on our network advantages.

We needed to reverse the mistakes we had been making on routes and schedules, aircraft size, and investment in passenger flight experience. We also needed to prove to investors that we had the operational competence to manage the capacity we already had. To do that, we needed to win the morale of our people; it takes employees who are enthusiastic and committed to doing a great job to achieve this moon-shot plan.

Until we had truly won back our employees who delivered that reliability, our growth plan wouldn't pass the laugh test.

Fortunately, the operational team led by Greg Hart began turning the corner in late 2016 and started to reestablish our operational prowess. We phased out tiny airplanes no one wanted to fly and added bigger, more spacious planes to the fleet, ones that could meet the needs of both frequent business travelers and the price-conscious passengers who may fly once a year. We could now offer a competitive Business Class experience in addition to expanding United Premium Plus, on top of Basic Economy. We took a different approach and designed our schedules so that that passenger had a larger variety of connection options, which then drove ever greater amounts of passenger traffic to flow through the hubs.

We were on course to deliver the best operational performance in United history.

Once again, employees came to the rescue of the airline. They weren't about to let the recent PR disasters define who they were and what they stood for as professionals.

It felt like employees had seen what United was going through with respect to the various crises in the news, and they lifted the whole organization onto their shoulders, as if to say to the world, "This is what United is really about." In the worst of times, our people had performed at their best, showing they had each other's backs.

By January 2018, we met again with investors, this time inside the historic New York Stock Exchange, and we knew our strategy would defy the conventional wisdom about how to run a profitable airline.

To understand why that was, we needed to explain to investors how United's network operated if we were going to really drive profits.

Think of a hub-and-spoke airline like United as if it were a manufacturing company. The product we manufacture is flight connections. The more connections we manufacture—the more customers we flow through each of our hubs to secondary destinations—the more profits the airline makes.

As a result of the merger, United undoubtedly held the most desirable hub positions, especially for premium international travel. Los Angeles (LAX) and San Francisco (SFO) provided the best gateways to the Pacific and Asia, while our hubs in Newark (EWR) as well as in Washington Dulles (IAD) provided the strongest routes to Europe. Stunningly, the seven hubs operated by United Airlines happen to account for 80 percent of all premium demand in the United States.

Additionally, our Star Alliance membership created a global network of connectivity that knitted together the best global airlines. For example, our routes between the East Coast and major destinations like Frankfurt, Munich, and London meant that Lufthansa customers could access mid-market US cities that Lufthansa could never serve directly by itself; conversely, United customers could connect through Lufthansa and other airline networks to reach foreign destinations that we couldn't directly serve. Similar partnerships with All Nippon Airways (ANA) and others created further connection-rich pathways for our customers across Asia/Pacific. Our Houston hub also provided a great gateway to Latin America and the Caribbean.

The problem: we had shrunk—or outright eliminated—our connections to small and midsize spoke cities around our hubs, where connections are really manufactured. Chicago, Denver, and Houston—with the latter two being among the fastest-growing cities in the United States—are strategically located, vibrant cities with some of the highest gross incomes in the country. Yet each was underperforming, with profit margins consistently 10 points below what our competitors were achieving in their mid-continent hubs at the time. In fact, we had pulled back our position in Denver over a number of years, which made no sense. This is a zero-sum game and if we stand still, we aren't saving money, we are losing market share and profits. When we shrink, our competitors only grow faster.

United had shrunk in small business markets and flew small regional aircraft while our network competitors flew large, more customer-friendly aircraft. They won the market. Why?

To appease investors, that's why. It was true, if paradoxical. Wall Street had punished United anytime the airline spoke out on growth, just as it had during our Q3 earnings call. It followed the conventional wisdom that growth drags down profitability. Yet it's precisely by following Wall Street's command to be more profitable that United wound up being, at the time, the least profitable of the major carriers.

The world has changed from ten years ago, when the most profitable routes existed between major destinations, such as Chicago to New York. Because of the entrance of low-cost carriers (LCCs), such as Southwest and JetBlue, as well as ultra-low-cost carriers (ULCCs), like Spirit, those types of routes are no longer as lucrative as in the prior decade. Instead, a regional route, such as Chicago to Bentonville, Arkansas, provides a higher yield because low-cost carriers do not have the right aircraft to serve it. Whoever has the right aircraft for that regional airport and service that feeds into a hub will win that crucial high-yield business.

We needed to wake Wall Street up to the fact that we were operating in a new environment, one where growth is the only way to improve earnings and remain competitive. We knew that after the previous earnings call, they wouldn't be content with mere assurances; they wanted us to nail our colors to the mast. And we did, by providing long-term "guidance"—forecasting—what investors could expect to earn during the years of growth. Usually, airlines had forecasted their projected earnings for only one year. We provided three years of projections, essentially promising that by 2020 investors could expect annual earnings of $11 to $13 for every share they owned. This was a 25 percent compound annual growth rate from the $7.50 in earnings per share expected for 2018.

I prepared the board for another drop in our stock and for Wall Street to reject this strategy at first. (Buckle your seat belts; we're in for a bumpy ride.) And that did happen. We saw a massive sell-off of United shares, with our stock dropping 12 percent in a single day, a spectacularly bad performance similar to the day of our 3Q 2017 earnings call.

Later that day, I found myself sitting on the trading floor of the New York Stock Exchange, being grilled on our strategy by industry expert and CNBC host Phil LeBeau and the on-air team of *Squawk on the Street*. As I stepped onto the set, my friend Jim Cramer, the bombastic host of CNBC's *Mad Money with Jim Cramer*, was stepping away after his own segment. He grabbed my arm and murmured in my ear, "I love you, Oscar, but I hope you know what you're doing!"

In the interview, Phil couldn't believe my sanguine attitude at the sudden drop in stock price. What did I have to say? I could only smile, shrug my shoulders, and reply, "I think it's a buying opportunity."

It was, I thought, the appropriate reply, though it may have sounded a little cavalier—Pollyannaish.

Turns out, we did know what we were doing and anyone who took me up on that advice would've been rewarded. Our stock rose from a nadir of around $63 per share, at the bottom of the sell-off that day, to a high of $96.70 by the end of November 2018.

Fast-forward to the fourth quarter of 2019. We had achieved what the analysts never believed we would, exceeding our projected three-year earnings per share guidance a full year earlier than expected.

• • •

In December 2019, less than two years after we announced our long-term earnings-per-share guidance, it was time to release my succession plan to the media.

Phil LeBeau was the first to report on *Squawk Box* that I would be departing as CEO of United Airlines in May 2020.

Co-host Becky Quick wondered aloud, "Oscar Munoz has been on a bit of a roll," referencing United's newfound winning streak. "I guess why take this move now?" she asked.

I couldn't help but be amused by how our turnaround strategy, which hadn't been given a chance at first, had so quickly become a given, its success foreordained. We had promised to narrow the profit margin gap to peers by growing the scale of our hubs, bolstering connectivity, and improving our asset efficiency. And, far ahead of schedule, my United family had fulfilled that promise and outperformed both large competitors on margin growth over those two years.

And we did it while flying more passengers than ever before in the nearly one-hundred-year history of United, all while achieving some of the best on-time performance ever for the company at all our hubs. United had rewritten the playbook for itself and the industry.

That's what I meant when I said, "Proof, not promise."

CHAPTER 17

LOCKDOWN

The president thanked the previous speaker as he turned in his chair and gestured in my direction. "Oscar?" Trump said, handing the floor over to me.

On March 4, 2020, the president had summoned my fellow airline CEOs and aviation industry leaders to an emergency meeting so that we could share our perspectives and recommendations on how the administration should address the growing crisis of COVID-19, which had already shut down China and most of Asia as well as Italy.

The flip side of being the largest gateway airline to the Asia/Pacific and to European regions was that our business was the most exposed of all US airlines to a downturn in those markets. When we saw demand dropping like a stone in the last days of February, we consulted public health experts. Many of them had been ringing the alarm for weeks, trying to alert policy makers to the coming storm, but to little avail. They told us just how bad it could get and the drastic changes in people's behavior that our industry would have to impose if we were going to keep flying at all. We knew that our actions would set the standard for other industries, and we got to work devising procedures to protect against this novel virus, which was still highly mysterious and deeply frightening.

My goal at the White House that day was twofold. First, I wanted to begin preparing the administration and the public for what was coming. Second, I sensed that our industry would soon have no choice but to ask for taxpayer support if we were going to survive. I needed to build goodwill and lay a predicate so that when that time arrived, the American people would have confidence that we had already done everything in our power to act responsibly and decisively in the public interest.

"I'll take a different angle," I began as the White House press corps, who were assembled around the walls of the Roosevelt Room inside the West Wing, swung their cameras and klieg lights and trained them on me.

"I look through this from a personal lens," I explained. "I'm a heart transplant survivor." I saw Vice President Pence nodding his head in the chair left of me, Trump sitting just next to him at the center of the giant oak table.

"If there's a poster child for the individual that could be affected by this, I'm it. And so, at United, we're exploring all the different ideas and aspects to ensure that our planes are as safe as possible," I said, turning to Dr. Robert Redfield, director of the Centers for Disease Control and Prevention, who was seated to my right.

When I flew into Washington, DC, that morning, instead of high-fiving employees and shaking hands as I usually do when walking the concourse, I reverted to simply fist-bumping. It was a callback to the days just after my transplant when my immune system was still fragile.

"We've invented the 'corona bump' at United, where you'll see us all fist-bumping each other," I said. I saw Trump chuckle. I had met with him several times in the past, both with the airline bosses and individually. I knew that when you find him in a receptive frame of mind, you don't squander the window of opportunity to get your message across.

"Anything," I emphasized to him, "that continues to project stability, calm . . . we need to adapt our behavior so that, indeed, we can continue to stay safe."

I tried to ignore the sounds of the camera shutters clicking incessantly as I spoke, and I felt the eyes of the entire global United family focused on me at that moment. I knew everyone was watching to see how I would keep myself and our company clear of the controversies that seemed to always swirl around the forty-fifth president and that administration, while also accomplishing what was needed to protect our business.

I was also hyperaware of the razor-fine line I had to walk politically, given the dire message I had to deliver.

"I don't recommend it," I replied, talking about my transplant experience.

"You have that one down. Don't recommend it," Trump cackled. "But you—hey, that's a fantastic story. Wow. That's great. Thank you very much, Oscar."

As the meeting broke up, we were escorted into the Oval Office for the obligatory photo op, though I knew how this picture would play politically with at least half of my employees—badly. That's when I noticed a woman standing on the other side of the ornate room; she didn't look up from her phone once. It took me a few seconds to put a name to the face—Kim Kardashian, who was there to personally lobby Trump.

That was just one of many surreal moments I witnessed during those early days of the COVID-19 pandemic, which would turn the world upside down, send shock waves through our industry and the broader economy, and change the course of all our lives forever.

• • •

The world had already changed from just a week earlier, when I was standing onstage at our annual leadership conference in Chicago, addressing thousands of our senior-level employees, from directors to the C-Suite.

It had been four years since I had made a surprise appearance at the same conference in 2016, only days after my heart transplant. Now I was speaking to the team I had assembled for the final time as their CEO. My weight had returned, and my urgency to continue unifying United was as robust as ever. I spoke about what I wished for United going forward as I prepared to hand day-to-day management of the company over to Scott Kirby in May 2020, when I would then assume the role of executive chairman of the board.

Of all the accomplishments we had achieved together during my tenure to rescue United from the precipice of failure and to turn around the company, I knew that the quality of the leadership team we had assembled would prove to be my most important and enduring.

"In all your travels," I asked the nearly two thousand colleagues assembled, "who's visited St. Paul's Cathedral in London?"

"The cathedral is, in part, the capstone of the project to rebuild London after the Great Fire destroyed the city in 1666," I explained. "A single architect, Christopher Wren, was tasked with raising the city from the ashes—brick by brick, block by block, building by building.

"If you stand at the center of that immense church," I said, having practiced my speech so I wouldn't choke up too much, "all that you'll see is a simple inscription celebrating his life's work but nothing else. The inscription reads: 'If you seek his monument, look around you.'

"If you want to know what I hope my legacy will be at United," I concluded, "look around you. You are the legacy."

I stepped off the stage, hugging everyone in the front row. The idea of social distancing was not yet a glint in our eyes, even though we knew something was happening in parts of our system that had already begun to affect demand in previous weeks. I made my way backstage, and I could still hear the applause in the auditorium. Our emcee, Mike Hanna, head of worldwide airport operations, was hyping up the crowd, telling them about our unstoppable momentum.

I walked into the greenroom and was met by grim looks on the faces of my executive team. It seemed our unstoppable force was about to hit an immovable object. While I was onstage, news had begun pouring in from across our operations. The buoyant mood of just twenty minutes ago, when I started my speech, had fizzled.

The COVID-19 pandemic had arrived.

We gathered around the conference table in the greenroom and held an emergency strategy meeting. Andrew Nocella—chief commercial officer, and one of the most gifted airline network strategists in the industry—told us that we were watching European demand drop like a stone, with bookings to Italy nearing zero. The only tickets being sold were to people trying to get the hell out of Dodge and reach the States before all of Europe locked down for God knew how long.

Soon, it was time for Scott to deliver his remarks. On the television feed being piped in from the auditorium, we listened as he spoke about our plans to continue growing the network, new aircraft purchases, hiring thousands of new employees, and how we would become the "best airline in the history of aviation."

Meanwhile, our team was already beginning to think about how we would begin to conserve cash by bringing down hundreds of routes, warehousing aircraft in fields in the desert, freezing all new hiring, and battening down the hatches.

It was as if the television feed was on a time delay and our employees in the auditorium were living in a different time zone from us.

Soon, the closing celebration in the main hall of the convention center started and the band began playing. But backstage we all knew the party was over. The tributes I had offered up to my team only a few minutes earlier would prove even truer than I could have imagined. In a matter of months, I would be stepping down as CEO. My legacy, the future survival of the New Spirit of United we had built—the future of United itself—would be in the hands of the team I had painstakingly put together over the past few years. They did not disappoint, as I knew they wouldn't.

Fire strengthens steel, as Scott likes to say. We had achieved "common metal," getting all our employees flying together on the same aircraft thanks to our constructive union negotiations. The COVID crisis would become a crucible moment for us to prove the mettle of our rebuilt culture. We set ourselves to work, trying to get our arms around the sheer scale of the problem confronting us.

Our team gamed out a series of scenarios to forecast what might happen to the business if demand dropped by 50 percent. Then 60 percent.

"Worst-case scenario," I wanted to know, "what would a 75 percent drop even look like?" The answer was clear: immediate bankruptcy. Ultimately, demand dropped by 93 percent for United.

We immediately began grounding planes, pulling down routes, and developing strategies to conserve cash. Knowing that we would start burning money at an exponential rate, Gerry Laderman and our financial operations team began laying the groundwork for going to the markets and raising liquidity.

I started working with Scott on a joint letter to employees. We needed to be honest—painfully so—with our people about what was about to happen. Sugarcoating the truth, and believing that hope might triumph over reality, wouldn't have won us any plaudits—and we were seeing too many rosy statements by CEOs and politicians who knew better, and their employees knew that they knew it, too.

One thing we could say, definitively, was that we would stand shoulder to shoulder with our employees every step of the way, starting with the two of us forgoing our salaries for at least a year. Eventually, all non-hourly management personnel accepted a 20 percent salary reduction. We explained that initially we would cut international service by 20 percent and domestic service by about 10 percent and place a freeze on what had been ambitious hiring plans.

The elephant in the room was the dreaded "F" word, "furloughs." We had made promises to our people, and we were determined to fulfill them. After all that we had done to re-earn the trust of our employees, we vowed that we would not backslide. We would do all in our power not to revert to the bad old days when management chose what ought to be the last-ditch resort as the first course of action whenever demand dropped.

The pride we had only recently felt in executing our growth plan and reaching our financial targets ahead of schedule quickly receded into dim memory once United became the first airline to withdraw its full-year earnings forecast.

A few days later, I was traveling through our hub at Washington Dulles (IAD). In a backroom office, I got on a conference call hosted by our industry's chief domestic lobbying group, Airlines for America (A4A), and I told them the results of our analysis. I urged my fellow CEOs to conduct similar ones for themselves. I recall at least one person on the call saying, "Oscar, we think this will pass."

I shook my head. "Look, I hear you that that number sounds dramatic, but it can't hurt to run the numbers."

I understood the source of their resistance. If I was right, then we would have no choice but to request taxpayer support, something anathema to airline CEOs. I knew they had the nightmare playing out in their minds of being hauled in front of Congress and seen as if they were looking for bailouts, just as the auto execs had infamously done in 2009.

The comparison simply didn't apply to the airline industry in early 2020. US airlines were in the strongest position they had ever been. Profits were high and cash reserves were strong. We were serving our customers well, delivering higher reliability while investing heavily in our planes, our people, and our product.

The US airline industry had not caused this COVID crisis, yet we were going to have to play a role in helping the country to survive it.

Taxpayer support would be essential because soon United's cash burn would rise to about $120 million per day. There's simply a limit to how hard and fast we can cut expenditures.

Airlines can't lay off employees and then hire them back when demand snaps back. If pilots, for example, don't stay in the air, their retraining could take months. If an airline gives up landing slots at airports to save money, there's no guarantee that it can just get them back. Aircraft aren't like the family station wagon that you can park in the garage for a few months and then just start it up again.

We began parking hundreds of aircraft in vast fields in the deserts of California and Arizona. But technicians and mechanics rarely go more than a week or so before they need to service and maintain those aircraft to keep them functional, a time- and labor-intensive effort.

If you recall, in 2022, pilot and crew shortages severely hampered the return to regular service, causing thousands of delays during peak travel season and infuriating customers. Had furloughs and layoffs been greater for a lack of payroll protection support, the industry might not have ever returned to normal. For sure, the US industry would be smaller, by orders of magnitude, with less competition, as airlines simply went out of business and aviation employees went to other sectors.

Let's also not forget, a functioning civil aviation system is vital to a formidable national security strategy as much as to a functioning economy. The military relies on US airlines to transport troops and personnel. The government required the airlift capacity of United and peer airlines for disaster relief, as well as for delivery of vital medical supplies and personnel at the height (or depths) of the pandemic.

To ensure their survival, US airlines needed to demonstrate a united front, something that's not natural to our industry. I felt like I was in *The Godfather*, trying to arrange an alliance between the five warring families. In fact, we would have to do something even more unprecedented and get all our unions onside as well.

I could already tell that the Trump administration would want to play down the crisis for political reasons and that would be a problem. If we were going to convince both Republicans and Democrats to stand behind our employees as demand dwindled, we would need to be honest about the size of the problem and demonstrate that we deserved the support of the American people.

"Look," I said on the call to my peers, "I urge you to look at that scenario of a seventy-five percent drop in demand, which we've done at United; when you do I think that you'll see my point."

That apparently did the trick.

When I met with President Trump during that March 4 meeting of airline executives, the cameras captured me holding my hands far apart to indicate the size of what United was seeing and the impact on our business. The *New York Times* carried the image on the front page.

The next hurdle came during a call hosted by the International Air Transport Association (IATA), with every single airline leader in the world present.

Despite our intense rivalry as companies, US airlines never competed with one another on safety and most of the leaders of the US airlines were in lockstep with me on our domestic industry's evaluation. Our close Star Alliance partner Lufthansa, led by Carsten Spohr, was also in agreement as were other key member airlines of IATA (International Air Transport Association). However, many of the international airline honchos in markets that had far less exposure to where the current COVID hot spots were located seemed very reluctant to receive the message. Like many, they were still in denial.

Over the next week, our government affairs team, led by Terri Fariello, a well-known Washington, DC, heavy hitter, whom I recruited in 2017, began coordinating efforts with the other US carriers as well as A4A to outline what kind of support the industry would require from the government so we could stay afloat and protect as many employee paychecks as possible.

As soon as we saw the gravity of the situation and the realization that the airlines would need federal funding to keep flying, one of the very first steps we took was to seek a meeting with Secretary of the Treasury Steve Mnuchin.

Terri Fariello arranged a meeting for Gerry Laderman, our CFO, and myself to meet with Mnuchin in his Treasury Department conference room. He cut to the chase—no niceties, which was just as well given the dire circumstances.

As we started to make our case for assistance, Mnuchin "got it" right away, understanding what we were facing as an airline industry and clearly appreciating the national security importance of maintaining a functioning US airline industry. I noticed him begin to scribble some numbers down on paper, and the math quickly rose to the $25 billion number our financial people had been discussing internally.

Though I didn't realize it at the time, that quick math planted the seeds of what would become the CARES Act (Coronavirus Aid, Relief, and Economic Security Act).

After that first meeting, we stayed in close touch with Mnuchin—he owned the policy portfolio—and, to his credit, he was always available to work through the many details, no matter the time of day or night.

Over the next several days my fellow airline CEOs and aviation leaders and I spoke with Secretary Mnuchin frequently, though we didn't always see eye to eye with him on the issue of whether support ought to come in the form of grants, loans, or warrants.

As we worked through this process with the administration, we also wanted to leverage our capabilities and provide all the assistance we could to support the United States' response. Soon, our airplanes were carrying vital personal protection equipment and medical personnel where they were needed most, free of charge.

The seven days after the March 4 White House meeting had a surreal "calm before the storm" quality to them. As we scrambled to reinforce the roof before the hurricane arrived, the rest of the world seemed to go on as if nothing extraordinary was happening. That all changed on March 11, 2020, a date that most people will remember as the start of COVID.

Every hour on that fateful spring day seemed to contain decades' worth of events. And with each hour, the world changed. Up until that point, this novel coronavirus seemed a world away, something that China was dealing with but wasn't of concern to Americans. That day, the reality of the crisis finally hit home, literally and figuratively. It rocked Wall Street as the Dow Jones Industrial Average fell 1,465 points.

New York followed the lead of companies in Seattle, where the first US cases were reported, and began sending employees home. Capitol Hill announced its first confirmed cases as Washington began shutting down. As the dominoes began falling faster, I remembered that line from Hemingway about how someone goes broke. "Gradually, then suddenly."

The NCAA announced that March Madness would be played without fans in attendance and the NBA suspended its season after a player tested positive, throwing that evening's game into a bizarre confusion that played out on live TV. The actor Tom Hanks and his wife announced they had tested positive and were being quarantined in Australia.

President Trump then delivered a prime-time address from the Oval

Office. As he concluded his remarks to the nation, he leaned back in his chair and, not realizing he was still being broadcast, let out a long, defeated sigh of "Okaayyyyyy."

By the end of the day, the United States had imposed a thirty-day ban on travel from Europe. The next morning, grocery stores were emptied by panicked shoppers; toilet paper became the coin of the realm.

CHAPTER 18

THE LAST ACT

My flight to Reagan National Airport (DCA) the following week, now mid-March 2020, was virtually empty, with the crew outnumbering the passengers aboard. The DC mayor had issued a general lockdown and shelter-in-place order while I was mid-flight. As we made our final approach, I looked out the window from the left side of the cabin down onto a Washington, DC, utterly transformed from the city I had left just a week earlier. Usually teeming with people at this time of year, the National Mall stretching out below us was deserted. The famous cherry trees that ring the Tidal Basin had bloomed a week early that year, but no one was there to enjoy them, save for those who had been summoned to help address the crisis.

I was greeted at the airport by Terri Fariello and we drove to the United offices, located a stone's throw from the White House. We knew we were in a race against time to secure a federal backstop to support the paychecks of frontline employees. I felt personally on the hook. I had devoted the past five years of my life to winning back the trust of my employees, assuring them that we would put their livelihoods first. The last thing I wanted for my final act as CEO was to betray that promise and preside over a gutting of the morale that we had worked so hard to build. We had scrambled our financial teams to find every lever possible to bring down spending and conserve cash.

By this time, the administration had introduced its infamous goal to get things back to normal by Easter. Every expert made it clear to us that this goal was not feasible. But it did provide us with an important argument. Without taxpayer support, the airline industry simply would not be there to help bring back the economy and make an "Easter miracle" possible.

At the United leadership conference back in February, we had announced $300 million worth of investments in customer-friendly improvements to our service. That was a distant memory now that demand had dropped by 93 percent and TSA was reporting that traffic through checkpoints had plummeted to only 8 percent of what it had been the previous year.

Our projections were indicating that we would serve as many passengers in an entire month as we did in a single day in 2019. There simply was no more fat left to cut before we started hitting bone and laying off frontline workers.

Terri and her team had been furiously lobbying both sides of the aisle, drawing upon years' worth of political capital.

At the end of one grueling day, after several hours of conference calls with lawmakers, I left our offices and walked toward the JW Marriott. I looked toward the White House and the Washington Monument beyond, the floodlights illuminating the monuments as dusk settled over the empty city.

The hotel, usually buzzing with activity, was a ghost town. Most staff had been sent home and housekeeping could not enter to change over the rooms. So each night we would have to switch rooms. Eventually, the hotel ran out of clean rooms, and we decamped to the historic Hay-Adams Hotel nearby.

On March 16, Airlines for America, led by Nick Calio, made a formal request of $50 billion in federal government assistance, that first meeting with Secretary Mnuchin providing the basis for negotiations.

Leaders of the industry—including Gary Kelly of Southwest, Robin Hayes of JetBlue, Brad Tilden of Alaska Airlines, Peter Ingram of Hawaiian Airlines, Doug Parker of American, and myself—so used to competing

188 | **Turnaround Time**

or negotiating against one another, now found ourselves hunkering down together in the offices of A4A—working the phones and making the case to lawmakers. As I think back on this event now, I am struck by the fact that this all-hands-on-deck effort to save the industry would mark the final acts for each of us as airline CEOs, a swan song to their employees for whom they cared deeply, each of whom would retire shortly thereafter, except for Peter Ingram and Robin Hayes, of course.

Call it the product of late nights and high-strung emotions, but in watching my fellow CEOs, as well as our union partners like Sara Nelson, work together, surrendering their egos but not their duties, I felt as much pride as ever to have belonged to this industry.

Our work was still far from done, and it was going to be another long night, except all the restaurants and grocery stores were either shut down or cleaned out of supplies. A member of Nick Calio's team at A4A volunteered to make a supply run to 7-Eleven to grab whatever snacks were still on the shelves. CEOs and union leaders of the industry sat around a conference table, eating junk food and drinking wine out of paper cups like a college bull session. The mood was serious, but there was a certain punch-drunk feeling after so many late nights. We knew that 750,000 of our colleagues, as well as their families, were counting on us for their livelihoods to get it right.

The price tag was sure to bring down a hail of criticism from all quarters.

The legislation had become larded with pork-barrel add-ons and was close to becoming dead on arrival, unless someone could step in and bring the Democrats and Republicans together.

The following evening—actually, it was closer to midnight—Doug Parker, CEO of American Airlines, and I stepped out of the room to join Sara Nelson, who was about to place a crucial call to administration officials.

Many benefits were derived from the long journey of repair with the unions. The greatest, certainly, was this united front we were able to show between management and labor on a matter of survival for our industry. My fellow CEOs and I knew that our hands were vastly strengthened because the counterparties on the other side of the table knew we had the backing of hundreds upon thousands of union members and their leaders. Once again, the unions rallied, organizing a concerted letter-writing and outreach campaign, calling upon their members to tell the elected leaders and administration officials we were dealing with to stand behind America's aviation professionals.

The outlines of the deal were within sight.

Some legislators were still calling for a significant number of riders to any proposed payroll protection package, many of which I agreed with, and United had already voluntarily made firm commitments to several of them. Senior leadership was already forgoing or significantly cutting salaries. A commitment to not furlough any employees as well as a guarantee that there would be no bonuses or share repurchases were table stakes, in my view.

At the time, only about twelve thousand of United's roughly ninety thousand employees were non-union white-collar jobs, and about 30 percent of those non-frontline employees were thinned out. We were going to be a smaller airline, unfortunately, but the pain would be felt starting at the top, not the front line.

The next crucial sticking point was whether the support would come in the form of direct grants that the airlines could pay back over time or loans, the terms of which were going to be extremely onerous and potentially self-sabotaging.

We continued to work the phones, and by one in the morning it looked like we were reaching the consensus needed to pass a bill that would provide a tranche of $25 billion in direct grants to be followed by another tranche of $25 billion in loans.

In the small hours of the night, I walked back to the Hay-Adams, but the doors were locked. I walked around the building a few times, looking for any sign of life. Had they shut down the hotel while I was out? I finally found a few hotel staff members standing outside a service door, taking a smoke break. They let me in, and I fell asleep the second my head hit the pillow.

• • •

On March 27, the president signed H.R. 748, the CARES Act, into law. Like the rest of the world, we did not yet know whether this milestone marked the beginning of the end of the crisis or only the end of the beginning. It turned out that light at the end of the tunnel was much further away than any of us had hoped.

The next two years we would continue to fight to protect our employees and customers while managing costs so that United would emerge from the pandemic stronger and intact.

As I write this, the airline industry is struggling to return to pre-pandemic levels of flying in order to meet the high demand of 2022. Airlines have returned to a position of strength, with profits rising, but so are prices. Tensions are rising, too. And my hope is that by writing this book, we can begin to comprehend one another and ease the pressures that we've seen reach a boiling point.

We saw many ugly scenes of unruly behavior on our planes during the pandemic, and it broke my heart to see our employees put in that position. Nevertheless, they performed with maximum grace.

I know that the frontline employees who are on the job, right now, will not forget the support offered to our industry in hard times. I hope that the public does not forget that the airline industry exists today only because of it. Whether the industry is thriving or not thriving, we are still flying. That is thanks to the thousands of people who marched into work when the world was marching in the opposite direction. They continued to serve when many of us had easier, safer options to work from home.

Employees were walking into the unknown, something that is easy to forget in hindsight, with the scientific information we now possess about the virus as well as effective vaccines. I recall during one of the first post-lockdown flights that I took, a fellow passenger remarked how good it felt to be back in the skies again.

"That's because so many of our frontline employees never left," I hastened to remind him.

Those employees will forever have my gratitude and the thanks of a grateful nation.

CHAPTER 19

FROM "WHAT'S WRONG?" TO "WHAT'S NEXT?"

May 2021 was approaching, and with it the planned culmination of my term as chairman of the board, as well as the end of my six years as a United employee. I had a clean bill of health and never felt better—and for once my doctors agreed. While my friends seemed to be slowing down, I felt an urgent need to speed up: a debt to repay, a loan of generosity from so many that I would need to make good for, and many promises yet to keep. No time like the present.

I had been granted so many gifts, a new heart most of all. I was not interested in allowing what I had learned during my years to rust and go to waste in a languorous retirement.

Teddy Roosevelt once remarked, "For us is the life of action, of strenuous performance of duty; let us live in the harness, striving mightily; let us rather run the risk of wearing out than rusting out."

For the first time in a long while, my next destination was unknown. I had spent the past six years focused solely on asking, "What's wrong?" and trying to fix it. Soon, I would have the latitude to ask myself, "What's next?" Not just for me, but also for the aviation industry.

It's been a half century since the world was introduced to a truly revolutionary aircraft. It's not too far a stretch to say that air travel today would still be pretty familiar to those members of the original jet-set generation from the sixties. I don't mean that in a good way. Despite fierce competition between airlines, the flying experience is not differentiated enough across airlines, in my view. The experience remains highly commoditized.

While the pace of innovation that marked twentieth-century aviation may not have stalled, it seems at least to be performing a "holding pattern." Meanwhile, every other industry continues to rapidly innovate, iterate, and reinvent itself, something aviation once seemed to do with regular ease.

The numbers don't lie.

It takes longer to fly the same number of miles today than it did in the 1990s, and last time I checked, the map hasn't changed. We have airplanes capable of much faster flight, but inefficiencies in our antiquated air traffic control system, designed for the 1950s and 1960s, slow them down to a crawl, as if they're souped-up Ferraris forced to drive on gravel roads.

More than sixty years since the first jet-powered transatlantic flight, it takes longer to fly from New York to London than it did in previous decades, and that's not because they retired the Concorde. The volatility of fuel costs plays a role here, as airlines have instructed pilots to slow down to save on fuel costs, which is yet another urgent reason United is leading the industry on the path away from fossil fuels toward a more sustainable future.

The trajectory of commercial aviation ought to be ever upward. Engineers and entrepreneurs alike by their nature do not accept what is true today for what will be true tomorrow.

We are due for another transportation revolution.

• • •

Happily, we are on the cusp of not one but several that will happen all at once, from the return of supersonic travel to the invention of sustainable fuel sources.

On a gray December morning in 2021, the excitement was palpable as that aviation future beckoned. To watch footage of the test flight that took place that day evokes memories of those grainy images of the Wright brothers' first flight at Kitty Hawk nearly 118 years earlier.

Only this time the world-changing event took place on the West Coast. As rain bounced off the carbon fiber airframe, the twelve rotors affixed to booms on the overhead wing ran nearly silent, like wind rustling through trees. Six of them tilted slightly back and forth as the operators tested the forward propulsion and steering. Then, as if it wished not to be bound to the tarmac for a moment longer, the all-electric aircraft became airborne for the first time, hovered a few minutes, and gracefully touched back down to whoops and hollers of celebration. One small step, but also a giant leap toward making advanced air mobility (AAM) a reality.

"This is a damn flying car!" I said to Archer Aviation's cofounder and CEO, Adam Goldstein, when he first took me to see the company's prototype aircraft. I remember Adam shot me a glance, as if to say, "What did you think we were building, a helicopter?"

I joined the board of Archer after United bet big on the company, choosing to back it over several rival start-ups. That investment made United the first airline to partner with an eVTOL (electric vertical takeoff and landing) aircraft company. Seeding it with a billion-dollar order for aircraft—with an option to purchase an additional $500 million more—United will soon operate a fleet of the consumer-rated aircraft, which Archer calls "Midnight."

When I visit Archer's HQ and meet with the designers, the room hums with the energy of a typical Silicon Valley start-up. The excitement is palpable as you walk through the open-plan office toward the garage in the back, where the prototype and flight-training simulator reside. The atmosphere that these aviation pioneers work in is a far cry from that of their predecessors' staid cultures, the ones who designed the great mass-market cars of the fifties and the jet planes of the early sixties—the buttoned-up engineers with their pressed shirtsleeves, pocket protectors, and horn-rimmed glasses.

Instead, this is an aerospace manufacturing company with the soul of a Silicon Valley start-up, complete with teams in tattered jeans, T-shirts, and hoodies. Whip-smart engineers and designers, mostly in their twenties, are hard at work trying to realize a vision that all of us have always had in our imaginations but has never existed in reality—a true flying car. They test, iterate, learn, and test again—moving as fast as their minds can work. They follow no road map, which makes sense because *"where they're going, they don't need roads"*—to paraphrase a 1980s movie that came out before most of them were born. Though they are tasked with building the safest flying machine in history, they're risk-takers at heart, which is why many of them turned down safer career paths at aerospace giants like Boeing, Airbus, and Lockheed, as well as at Silicon Valley darlings like Google, Apple, and Tesla.

And as Adam tells me about how Archer will change the way we live and work, allowing people to fly over the traffic, I can think back to what it was like to grow up in Los Angeles and lament the vast amounts of my life that I've spent stuck in the concrete confines of the 405 or the 101. For an airline CEO, the drive to the airport is the most onerous part of any journey. It's also the part I have absolutely no control over. For example, Houston and Denver are two of the fastest-growing cities in the United States, with astonishingly long drive times. The car ride from Chicago's downtown financial district to O'Hare can be as quick as twenty-five minutes or as long as ninety minutes, with little predictability.

If we can make the first part of your journey seamless, stress-free, and safe, then your experience once on board a United plane will be phenomenally enhanced. Imagine the economic multiplier effect that results from closing the gulfs that exist between exurban and urban, rural and metropolitan populations. Imagine living in a world not being constrained by traffic—a world where you can travel from Manhattan to JFK in just ten minutes, or LAX to Downtown L.A. in just seven minutes.

Airports and the cities that govern them were ill prepared for the previous ground-based ride-share revolution of Lyft and Uber. Many initially hesitated to invest in creating special lanes, which then caused traffic and safety nightmares at the pickup and drop-off zones.

Airports, airlines, and regulators—we all need to get ready for what will become the most important transportation revolution since the automobile. Electric flight is coming, and with aircraft like Midnight, it will be quiet, efficient, clean, and affordable. There will come a day, and it's not so far off, when someone in downtown Chicago, for example, summons a UAM service to fly from their neighborhood mini airport or vertiport to the vertiport located curbside at O'Hare—for the cost of a ground-based ride-sharing service today.

And if that vision is enough to blow your hair back, get ready to be pushed back in your seats by the force of the coming supersonic aviation revolution.

• • •

The blazing sun of the Mojave Desert bounced off the sleek aerodynamic airframe, as the Boom team prepared for its latest test. Seventy-five years after Chuck Yeager and his bullet-shaped, orange X-1 rocket plane streaked across the same Mojave skies in 1947, Boom Supersonic proved that it, too, had "the Right Stuff" by testing its own XB-1 prototype plane.

At sixty-eight feet long, with a seventeen-foot wingspan, a symphony of carbon fiber composites, elegant control surfaces, envelope-pushing aerodynamics, propelled by powerful J85-15 engines, Boom's XB-1 supersonic demonstrator, dubbed "Baby Boom," serves as a $1/3$-scale test article designed to inform the company's signature supersonic airliner *Overture*.

Though pioneering in every way, *Overture* feels like a blast from the past—an ode to the future we dreamt of but never had. Just five years after Boeing built its first jetliner in 1958, people thought supersonic flight would soon become the standard form of commercial air travel. Since the retirement of the Concorde in 2003, however, most of us have regarded the arrow-thin plane that landed in a distinct, high-nosed swan dive as one of those romantic but impractical ways of getting around. It was something beautiful to behold, sure, but so expensive that the economics couldn't support the glamour and the technology couldn't overcome the vice attached to its virtue: the sonic boom.

Overture is the spiritual successor to the Concorde. Like all heirs to a great legacy, this aircraft will pick up where its predecessor left off. Thanks to a combination of computer simulations and wind-tunnel testing, revolutionary materials engineering, and state-of-the-art engines that ditch afterburners, combined with 100 percent sustainable fuel, *Overture* is not only an improvement on the Concorde but also sustainable in every way that the Concorde was not—economically and environmentally. Scheduled for commercial use in 2029, the aircraft will transport passengers twice as fast as the fastest airliner, reaching blistering speeds of Mach 1.7: Los Angeles to Sydney in eight and a half hours rather than fourteen and a half hours. New York to London in just three and a half hours rather than six and a half hours. San Francisco to Tokyo in six hours, rather than more than ten hours today.

United made the world's first purchase agreement for this revolutionary aircraft, with an initial order of fifteen and options for thirty-five more. With both the civil and defense partners lining up on its taxiway, Boom is proving that there is a strong and broad market demand for supersonic transport.

"We believe that life is better lived in person," says Boom founder and CEO, Blake Scholl. "Our mission at Boom is to make the world dramatically more accessible. Sustainable supersonic travel enables three-day business trips to become one-day hops, long-distance relationships to thrive, and humanitarian missions to save more lives."

• • •

Whenever I visit the headquarters of Archer or Boom, I am exhilarated to see the future taking shape in front of my eyes. Archer's refinement of battery technology and Boom's development of alternative fuels for supersonic flight are propelling us toward the most important revolution of all: a sustainable future, for aviation and our planet.

As with any truly important technological revolution, there must be a prime mover, an entity that commands the scale to create demand and kick-start a market. In the 1950s, a northern California–based company, Fairchild Semiconductor, received government contracts that led to the invention of the first integrated silicon circuit by 1960. Thus, Silicon Valley was born, leading to tech booms and the information revolution. Beginning in 1973, it was DARPA (Defense Advanced Research Projects Agency), the Defense Department's venture-capital arm, that funded the experimental technology that led to the development of the early internet, as well as core technologies like GPS. Henry Ford created the mass market for affordable family-owned cars, and we know the impact Tesla has had on pushing the entire auto industry toward electric vehicle production.

During my tenure as CEO, our team tried to trigger a race for sustainable fuel production, believing it to be the only way to create a market demand sufficient to justify building the infrastructure necessary to scaling its production, its distribution, and, ultimately, its consumption at airports around the world.

In 2018, our team put United on record as the first US airline to commit to reducing our carbon footprint by half by 2050, the crucial date set out by the Paris Climate Accords. We invested early in pioneering start-ups like Fulcrum Bioenergy, which is working on bringing new refining techniques to scale. After several years of investment, by 2019 United Airlines represented more than 50 percent of the entire industry's purchase of sustainable biofuels. That was a bold move at the time, and while I was a strong evangelist for the business and moral case for making these types of long-tail investments in new technologies, my successor Scott Kirby has made it his personal crusade, racing ahead to make United the first 100 percent "green," carbon-neutral airline by that crucial 2050 timeline.

United is going beyond reducing its carbon footprint at the margins and seeding technologies that will initiate humanity's next industrial revolution and leave our dependence on fossil fuels where it belongs: in the past.

• • •

"Fuel hedging" is a term that, for decades, became synonymous with airline management. Walk a few blocks from my office in Chicago's Loop and you'll find yourself in front of the Chicago Board of Trade. There, from the depths of the trading pits, futures contracts on fuel and other commodities were purchased. Since the 1980s, airlines would spend inordinate amounts of effort and resources calculating how best to lock in a good fuel price or to reduce exposure—to hedge—against a potential spike.

But times change, as they should. Today the infamous trading pits, where hundreds of brokers would jostle and shout over one another to execute trades in a manic frenzy, are quiet. The Chicago Mercantile Exchange replaced the old "Open Outcry" model with sophisticated electronic trading systems. Save for the guided tours that pass through them, the pits sit empty, relics of a big, boisterous bygone era of boom-and-bust.

I firmly believe that United's dependence on fossil fuels must go the way of the trading pits and become a relic of aviation antiquity as the industry races toward a fully sustainable future.

As I arrived as CEO, hedging was limping out the exits as a core business practice for most airlines, especially United. The philosophy behind this decision was simple. We aren't banks. Our business should depend on smart management, disciplined finances, and customer loyalty—not betting our business on the market and hoping we've covered our bets.

Our two most costly uncertainties are weather and fuel.

If only I could hedge against good weather out of O'Hare. But what I can do is reduce our dependence on fossil fuel; it's the smartest hedge there is. We spend more on fuel than on ground operations, facilities, and landing fees combined. I've seen fuel cost us anywhere between $15,000 and $30,000 every minute. I have no idea what that cost will be at the time you're reading this, and that's the point. Fuel price volatility lies at the heart of the business case I make on behalf of sustainability.

The airline that can spend less on fuel, our most volatile cost by far, is the airline that can afford to spend more on customer-winning innovations. It is the airline that can plan for the future, not fearing to be knocked off its strategy by a price spike.

Between 1990 and 2020, which is an important period by which the aviation industry benchmarks its progress, United had improved by more than 45 percent on fuel efficiency. But efficiency will not be enough to outpace aviation's growing share of global emissions as billions more people enter the middle class and take to the skies. Jet fuel demand is expected to double by 2050, outpacing whatever progress we're currently making. The International Air Transport Association projects air passenger traffic to double within two decades. More than eight billion people will be flying every year, forcing emissions to skyrocket 300 percent to 700 percent by 2050.

It should be said that buying and selling carbon credits offers no permanent solution. It doesn't reduce the carbon from the source of the emission, nor does it curb demand for fossil fuels. Even if the entire global aviation sector were permanently grounded today, the number of coal plants being built in India and China would dwarf aviation's contribution to global warming. Carbon offsets sound great on press releases and speeches, but they are little more than pretense.

Yet even now, in private conversations with some of the biggest capital allocators in our society, the argument is often dismissed as alarmist, "tree hugging," and—above all—costly. If the cost of transitioning away from fossil fuels is high, consider the costs of inaction.

If you chart the doubling of global flights in a graph along with the growth of warming, they intersect at the year 2050. This is a game of miles, not inches.

We can begin to glimpse the future that our grandchildren will live in when they become adults. We still have a few seconds before midnight to make it a brighter one.

We no longer have time for Potemkin solutions or "greenwashing." Old corporate platitudes about climate change will no longer do. Politicians and corporations can no longer lie to others or to themselves. Our industry can no longer wait for governments or other entities to impose regulations upon us before we make strong cases for sustainability to our boards and shareholders.

It is agreed among 99.9 percent of scientists that climate change is mainly caused by human activity, and finally a majority of Americans agree. In April 2022, the Pew Research Center found that three-quarters of Americans now believe climate change is man-made. That's an increase from just 27 percent of adults in the United States in 2016. In some ways, the problem threatens to reverse itself. If disbelief in man-made climate change led to apathy in the past, then a fatalistic pessimism that nothing can be done to address it will lead to an apathy that will seal our fate. The same Pew Research poll found that more than half of American adults (53 percent) no longer believe the world can avoid climate change's worst impacts. It is the rare opinion shared by both sides of our political divide.

We need not submit to such a defeatist attitude, and when I look at this array of human ingenuity being applied to perhaps the greatest problem ever confronted, I take a much-needed measure of hope. As President John F. Kennedy said at American University in 1963, speaking of the nuclear arms race and hopes for peace in the cold war, "Our problems are man-made, therefore, they can be solved by man. And man can be as big as he wants. No problem of human destiny is beyond human beings. Man's reason and spirit have often solved the seemingly unsolvable—and we believe they can do it again."

The gendered language may seem a bit dated, but the message is as relevant as ever.

Fortunately, we already know how to achieve sustainable fuel, and we are seeding new technologies. I am impressed every day as I see our United team pushing new technologies that seem ripped from science fiction and are beginning to bring SAF (sustainable aviation fuel) to market at an industrial scale.

Right now, we have in our possession the technologies needed to make aviation a leading industry for clean energy innovation; we just need the right market incentives in order to bring them to scale.

By acknowledging that the threat posed by climate change is primarily man-made, we have it in our power to fix it. Carbon pollution and global warming are the result of two hundred years of human endeavor, from the industrial revolution onward. If the problem itself is the product of our genius, then it will be human beings' collective genius that will solve it, once and for all.

AFTERWORD:
NO DIRECTION HOME

As planned, in May 2020 I formally transitioned to the role of executive chairman, handing the CEO role to Scott Kirby. When we devised our transition plan, I had hoped that the final months of my tenure at the top would be a coda to my first thirty-seven days. I wanted to travel the system and personally thank as many of our people as possible. I wanted to tell them what their faith and hard work had meant to our success, and to me personally. I wanted to remind people that though times seemed very dark, this, too, would pass. However, it was perhaps more fitting that after working for years to build the "New Spirit of United," my final act as CEO would be to keep it alive in its moment of maximum peril.

If you remember, the morning I received the call that I would be receiving my heart transplant was the morning we set forth the future of the company. The last thing I told my team before heading to the hospital was "I'll see you on the other side."

My own survival that morning was still in doubt, but because of the choice we made to put employees first, United's future was secured. When I bid farewell as CEO, even though we were still in the depths of the pandemic, I retold that story and compared it to the moment we now faced. I reassured everyone, "I will see you on the other side."

As you might imagine, the flight deck of an airplane demands precise protocols and routines. For instance, the captain always hands control over to his copilot by declaring, "You have the control." Only when the pilot beside him concurs, "I have the control," does the captain allow himself to take his hands off the wheel, knowing that the aircraft is in safe hands. No good captain hands control over when a plane is in danger, only in calm skies and in an orderly way. Air traffic control may then ask the pilot to state his intentions, announcing where he intends to steer the aircraft next.

To say that the United Airlines I handed off to Scott in May 2020 had been transformed from the one I took over in 2015 wouldn't be totally accurate. Instead of a departure from the past, the New United we built signaled a return of something tried and true. The company that had pioneered commercial air travel with the first transcontinental passenger flight inaugurated the jet age with the first jet-powered service—the airline that more than any other had opened the skies to the everyday traveler and that had coined the term "The Friendly Skies" was finally restored to its rightful place.

In one of my final acts as CEO, I traveled to our flight training center in Denver, near the old Stapleton International Airport, the largest training facility of its kind in the world.

One of the greatest privileges of running an airline is to be invited to participate in what's called "captain upgrades," officially acknowledging that an aviator has made that move from the right-hand seat to the left-hand seat that belongs to the captain. It's a matter of inches, but it takes the span of a career to traverse. As I pinned captain wings onto those aviators, one of our training officers told me about an old saying.

"A first officer can always look to his or her left and receive help or assurance from the captain. But, once you upgrade to the captain's seat, you look to your left and see only your own reflection in the window." The same is true of any leadership position, especially as CEO. Like a flight crew, we all work together. But there comes a time when you can rely only on your own convictions and belief in the values that got you there in the first place.

There were many moments like that during my tenure at the top of United: The moment before I went under anesthesia for a heart transplant. The dark night of self-reflection before opening myself up on national television, knowing that the world wouldn't be judging my actions as a business leader but my character as a human being. The countless quiet exchanges with my fellow employees as they shared with me the hardships they were going through in their lives.

Though I am not avowedly religious, I confess there were private moments when I fell to my knees in prayer or contemplation, to borrow Lincoln's phrase, simply because I had nowhere else to go. But even in those lonely moments of leadership, I never felt truly alone. I knew there were tens of thousands of fellow human beings who were part of this United team, who were in it for the long haul with me, come what may.

They saved my job and restored my faith in myself more times than I can count. Had they not had my back and not voiced loud support for my return rather than replacement, my tenure as CEO would have ended the day of the heart attack. Their letters made me realize not only that I could still do the job but that I would fight for the job when investors tried to take control of the company. Their work ethic and dedication to each other made me confident that if I bet on them, they would make our growth plan successful, returning United back to profitability and success.

I joined United to change it. In the end it changed me. I prided myself on taking care of my employees, but in truth they were the ones who cared for me.

As I handed control over to Scott, allowing him to state his own intentions for the airline, I knew I was leaving my employees in good hands. And I was leaving him in good hands as well—theirs.

Even now, in all my countless flights with the United family, I always try my best to be the final person to depart toward the gate area. It's often my best chance to enjoy priceless moments with our team and crews— from ticket counter to the break room, the ramp to the gate.

I get to witness the flawless teamwork in action, as they orchestrate countless moving pieces with precision, all to make the magic of our flights happen. I always look for the touching wave of the jet bridge driver to the passengers and crew as they pull away from the plane, signaling the start of a new journey.

But for all of us who make those journeys possible, we know we never say goodbye. Not to each other. Not really.

In fact, as we know, saying goodbye is forbidden as bad luck, going back centuries, on the seas as well as in the skies.

That wave as the plane pulls away, marking yet another successful turnaround, really means, "Until we meet again."

. . .

It's a fairly short flight from Los Angeles to Mexico City, the bookends of my life story: the place where I was raised and the country where I was born.

The hop takes roughly three and a half hours, faster if the tailwinds favor you.

Of course, the experience of traveling back to Mexico at this stage of my life is a far cry from what it took to travel in the opposite direction, once upon a time, immigrating to the United States as a child.

T. S. Eliot wrote, "The end of all our exploring will be to arrive where we started and know the place for the first time."

That is certainly the sentiment I felt as we made our final descent into Benito Juárez International Airport during my first post-pandemic flight to Mexico City in the spring of 2022.

I tend to work during flights, but this time I found myself glued to the view afforded by my window seat through the journey, watching the landscape rolling by, miles beneath us. When you're at cruising altitude, all seems at peace and no borders are visible from the skies, only the thin gravel roads that demarcate the boundaries of one cattle ranch or share-cropper farm from those of its neighbors.

I cast my mind back and tried to trace, in reverse, the long, winding path my family took many decades ago, in fits and starts, along our journey to reach Los Angeles and ultimately settle in the United States as American citizens.

I thought of the people I met along the way who shaped that journey and who shaped me.

As we emerged through the cloud cover, Mexico City began to reveal itself, gradually unfurling its vast expanse and stretching as far as the eye could see.

I love this immense city. It thrums with energy. Every time I'm here my heart—the miraculous gift of a heart transplant—begins to beat a little faster.

Of course, when I think of the nearly seven long years and all that transpired between this moment and those early days at United, my heart beats faster still.

And as I think about the way my personal survival and United's revival unfolded in parallel, while it may prove too much to say that those two stories could not have happened separately, it's impossible not to appreciate how they certainly rhymed.

ACKNOWLEDGMENTS

It seems fitting to end this book in the same spirit with which I began it—with gratitude.

When friends had kindly read these chapters in manuscript form, they asked whether certain people mentioned are composite characters—the product of artistic license and dramatic storytelling—or if they are real. I understand why they ask. Some people who played a role in this story seem too good to be true, I know.

The fact is that each and every person mentioned in this book is real and genuine in every sense of the word—from the employees whom I credit with the genesis of United's turnaround to my family, who shaped my personal growth in life, to the friends and colleagues who gave me guidance and purpose along the way, and to so many others who perhaps never knew the impact they had upon me until now.

Yet at the same time, many of them are indeed composite characters, at least in a sense, because they are representative of so many others who deserve to be thanked and celebrated but who didn't fit neatly into the chronology or narrative structure of this book. To their credit, United employees whom I've specifically profiled agreed to be highlighted only as long as I made it clear to the reader that they stand in for thousands of their colleagues, in the United family and across aviation, who share their values and professionalism.

It was simply impossible to mention everyone, yet I appreciate the opportunity to include a few more names here.

• • •

To my colleagues who served as my chiefs of staff during the latter part of my tenure:

Julie Stewart took over from Mandeep Grewal and did a brilliant job. A former leader of our investor relations team, her financial acumen and political acuity proved essential to effectively communicating United's profitability and growth trajectory in 2018.

She was succeeded by Nathan Lopp, who has since gone on to become vice president of corporate real estate, a critical leadership position. Having had many people serve as chief of staff before him, I can say, definitively, I've never seen this type of role performed better. His tenure proved the longest of anyone in that job, and he continues to reflect everything that I admire and value most in a corporate leader. Along with Jamie Smith, my longtime executive assistant, he has become like family to me.

Natalie Mindrum, who took over the role in 2020, agreed to undertake double duty by assisting me during my tenure as chairman while also performing her other full-time job as managing director of regional strategies. In 2021, Max Slutsky did an equally masterful job in supporting me while also serving as director of Strategic Advocacy and Planning at our offices in Washington, DC, up until my retirement that spring.

Each of them brought unique qualities to this role; all of them became trusted counselors and close friends.

Howie Shapiro, founder of Head Coach, a leadership development consultancy, helped me to become a better leader and stronger executive over the course of our many years of friendship. His expertise has helped hundreds of aspiring leaders, including me, take giant leaps in their careers.

I owe thanks to Scott Weiss, CEO and global managing partner at Speakeasy, a consultancy that helps leaders develop their communications and presentational skills. I have directed hundreds of individuals to Speakeasy, and his book, *Dare!*, is required reading for anyone who aspires to become a more effective leader and communicator. It was the book I read right before taking on the role as CEO of United Airlines, and it helped me articulate my own approach to leadership.

To the outstanding members of the United Corporate Communications team, who often go unsung, let me sing their praises here. I'm especially grateful to Megan McCarthy, Dana Brooks Reinglass, and the individual members of their team.

Maggie Schmerin, now head of Global Advertising and Social Media, has taken up the torch of the "New Spirit of United" and lifted it to new heights, demonstrating each day how "good leads the way."

This team has carried on telling the story of United with a sense of purpose and joyful enthusiasm that make me proud every time I come across their work—in print, in broadcasts, and on billboards around the world.

That's certainly true of everyone who served on UA's Creative Services team, led by Mick Masuka, including Johnny Walker, Siri Berting, and Sara Mays.

I am especially grateful to them for creating the photo that graces the cover of this book, as well as the wonderful employees whom it features: Alvohnnette Lee, Kevin Nakamoto, George Rencher, Sean Bowen, Margarita Isabel Nery, Issa Charroux, Jennifer Brown, Willie Romero, Laura Quiles, Megan Polo, Norman Nanstiel Jr, Earnest Quattlebaum, and Aina Kam (Shane Aina Kekulana Kam).

Among those visual storytellers, I am indebted to Joe Lammerman. He joined United as a ramp agent more than twenty-five years ago, but later found his calling and became the permanent in-house photographer at our Chicago O'Hare hub. I will always admire Joe's eye for finding a great shot, the way he captures moments and their meaning, to bring something magical out of the everyday workings of an airline.

There are many other segments of the United family who not only made the events of this book possible but freely offered their time and effort to assist the project itself. I am especially indebted to Michael

Leskinen, president, United Airlines Ventures, and his colleague Kristina Munoz (no relation), director of Investor Relations, who contributed their expertise to a key section of the book.

• • •

During my tenure, I worked closely with the leaders of several large financial institutions—including investment banks, whose work contributed to our success, among them Morgan Stanley, Evercore, and JP Morgan Chase, as well as world-renowned consultancies, especially Boston Consulting Group and McKinsey Partners.

In addition to Richard Edelman's communications firm, I relied mightily on the strategic advisory firm Brunswick, founded by Sir Alan Parker, who went out of his way to spend time with me personally, reflecting the importance of United's success to the global economy. Jayne Rosefield is the founding partner and head of Brunswick's Chicago office. There is simply no one more gifted at helping CEOs and organizations create, align, and communicate strategic initiatives than her.

I am a former member of the Business Roundtable, led by Josh Bolten, and the Business Council, led by Marlene Collucci—both influential associations of CEOs. I commend the way these groups responded to the upheavals in 2020—the pandemic, the racial strife that followed, and the painful realities they revealed about our society.

• • •

Like many before me, I failed terribly in my attempt at retirement by quickly joining a diverse range of corporate, civic, and philanthropic boards of directors, as well as several entrepreneurial endeavors whose missions are close to my heart.

I joined the board of directors of Salesforce in 2021, drawn to the company by the quality of its leadership and the collaborative culture instilled by its founder, Marc Benioff. From his apartment in San Francisco, he launched a new subscription-based model that disrupted an industry and delivered unprecedented value to its customers and stakeholders. *Forbes* has called him the "innovator of the decade," and *Fortune* has called him one of the world's twenty-five greatest leaders. I am proud to call him a colleague and a friend.

As a board member of CBRE Group, the commercial real estate services and investment company, I would like to applaud the leadership of the firm's president and CEO, Bob Sulentic, for cementing the firm's place at the forefront of its industry, thanks to a relentless focus on growth and high-quality service to its clients.

As an independent trustee on Fidelity's Equity and High-Income Funds board, I am grateful to its leadership for their firm commitment to excellence and a dedication to the principles that make our economy work better and for more people.

I joined the board at Archer Aviation and invested in the vision of its CEO, Adam Goldstein, because I believe in this company's ability to be the first to successfully develop a safe, commercially viable flying car that will revolutionize travel. I believe that the future of flight must be sustainable and affordable, and the Archer team—in partnership with United Airlines—will be the ones to help us reach that destination.

I also wish to recognize the work of my fellow trustees and President Carol Folt at the University of Southern California, as well as at the Brookings Institution, and I am proud to be included among the members of the Defense Business Board, which leverages the expertise of the private sector to help the Pentagon protect our national security interests and fulfill our sacred obligations to service members and veterans.

I joined the board of Univision just as it merged with Televisa, which created the first fully integrated Spanish-language media company, delivering high-quality original programming to more than 100 million households every day, including more than 60 percent of TV audiences in both the United States and Mexico.

This market represents the last truly "open lane" in the global streaming battle, and I credit the leadership of CEO Wade Davis for uniting these two richly loved brands to create this new player that will reshape the media scene. The most important and lasting story that will come out of TelevisaUnivision's dream factory, perhaps, will be the way the company itself contributes to the overall success story of Spanish-language culture, which will be transformative for generations to come.

I cannot express sufficient admiration for Sol Trujillo and Gary Acosta, my partners in many endeavors. We've worked together on building the Latino Donor Collaborative, a research arm focused on analyzing the economic and social contributions of Latino and Hispanic Americans; the annual L'Attitude Conference, which has become the largest and most important gathering of Latino leaders in the nation; and Lat VC, an investment fund aimed at catalyzing investment into high-growth start-ups led by Latinos and Latinas. In combination with my investment and work on the board of TelevisaUnivision, the world's leader in Spanish-language programming, we are dedicated to changing the narrative and explaining exactly how vital the Latino and Hispanic community is to America's twenty-first-century economy.

Nancy Brown, CEO of the American Heart Association, as well as her colleague Brian Shields, are valued partners to me. Together, we've expanded the reach of the AHA's Social Impact Funds, which make strategic investments to social entrepreneurs working hard to improve long-term health outcomes in the most underserved communities.

To that end, I am especially proud of the work being developed by my associates at Cleerly. Founded by James K. Min, MD, this team is inventing predictive precision heart technology that uses artificial intelligence to better diagnose and treat patients who are at risk of heart disease. It is a technology that, if it had existed then, would have alerted me to my risk, likely even averting it altogether.

Today, usually when I am traveling through airports, perfect strangers will approach me in the terminal or tap me on the shoulder while passing my seat on a flight and explain how hearing about my story of cardiac survival inspired them to get checked or to call 911 as a precaution. Sometimes they tell me that my story gave them the strength to get better, just as the example of my fellow patients gave me hope when it grew scarce. "It saved my life," one person told me, tears welling in the eyes as we stood in the terminal.

In the opening chapters, I wrote that if this book could raise awareness and save even one life, it would have been well worth it. Interactions like these have convinced me that it was, indeed.

Ironically, I travel our service even more after stepping away as CEO to pursue these various post-United projects. To organize it all into a strategic, integrated whole, I've established Polaris Limited Partners, a name that nods to United's premier international product.

Making this hectic post-CEO life viable is Ashley Prietsch, a stellar executive assistant, whose tireless professionalism has kept this book and my many post-United endeavors on track. If you happen to see me at the airport, and I'm on time, it's thanks to Ashley's (seemingly) effortless ability to multitask and troubleshoot—and she does so with admirable grace.

Allison Landry is a valuable adjunct to this small team. In addition to providing me with expert counsel on a variety of subject matter, she kindly lent her keen editorial eye to improving several chapters of this book.

• • •

Had I chosen to write a full-blown memoir, rather than a book dedicated specifically to United's turnaround, the previous chapters would be filled with tributes to so many friends and colleagues—from AT&T to Coca-Cola to Pepsi. When I joined US West, for example, its CFO, Al Spies, took me under his wing, becoming a mentor and remaining a close friend to this day.

To my friends and colleagues at CSX, those whose careers have since led them to new places and those who still lead the railroad today, I will be forever grateful for banding together, despite the odds, to create a thriving company and a rewarding place to work. I hope from this book they begin to glimpse the full extent of their legacy and how the lessons I learned from them have lived on—at United, as well as at the companies and organizations I have since worked with.

My college years at USC were formative, owing as much to the world-class faculty at the Marshall School of Business as to the influence of my classmates and fraternity brothers, or the "Chee Boys"—a self-ascribed name we choose—or refuse—to leave behind.

In addition to Scott Frisbee, who plays a role in this book, I would not have survived those "lean years" during college without Alan Boring. The three of us met in the first weeks of our freshman year and we remain just as we were then—the best of friends—and I thank them for being the kindest of human beings.

I would be remiss if I failed to mention Dave Brown and Lawrence Amaturo, another pair of friends who shaped my trajectory in life. We met in those heady days, post-college, when the future was endless and so was our energy. Though time has made us a little grayer with each passing year, our friendship has only strengthened. Our many trips together have become important milestones, marking the stages of our careers and the growth of our families.

. . .

United's survival story had many authors, and so did my own. The doctors, nurses, and EMTs, the pre-op and post-transplant coordinators, and the staff members of Northwestern Medicine's Bluhm Heart Hospital and the Rehabilitation of Chicago have my undying gratitude. As does Byoung Lee, whose expertise in physical training and rehabilitation speeded my recovery. He continues to be a constant source of inspiration as well as perspiration, of mental and spiritual support to me and to our entire community in Jacksonville, Florida.

I must give a special tribute to Jenny Whitlock, who was then a volunteer at the hospital. She basically adopted my family during those long days and nights when I first arrived at the hospital. She has since become an honorary part of my family, and I will forever cherish what she did to lighten those dark days and to make every day we've known her since become brighter still. My friend Blake Wilson also deserves credit for the support he lent to our family during that time. I want to pay tribute to the staff of the apartment building where I live in Chicago, who showed so much kindness to us, as well.

Though I am a recent transplant (excuse the pun) to the city, I must give my endless love to the City of Big Shoulders for welcoming me with open arms. I especially admire the community of civic leaders represented by the Economic Club of Chicago and World Business Chicago.

Our house in Ponte Vedra, Florida, remains, as ever, our family's home base, and where our fondest memories continue to be made. Alongside nearby Jacksonville, the community welcomed us with open arms many years ago, and I take pride in seeing how the business and philanthropic communities there have elevated themselves to national, even international, stature.

· · ·

There were many people who helped me through this unfamiliar writing process. I am forever grateful to my editor, Hollis Heimbouch, of Harper Collins, as well as Kirby Sandmeyer; their erudition and empathy transformed a crude manuscript into a true narrative, and they steadfastly supported my vision of writing a memoir focused not on myself but on others. My thanks to Jim Levine, founder of Levine-Greenberg-Rostan Literary Agency, and Greg Shaw, founder of Clyde Hill Publishing, who served as my "book sherpas" guiding me up this steep climb as a first-time author— sometimes carrying me on their shoulders when I lost my way. I owe my thanks to Tom Rosshirt, who advised me early on, as well as to our mutual friend, Dr. Timothy Shriver, founder of UNITE. As chairman of the board of the Special Olympics, Tim and I forged a partnership between United Airlines and the Special Olympics, an organization whose mission profoundly aligns with our airline's shared purpose of "connecting people and uniting the world."

To the one storyteller who has been with me since the beginning, Brian DeSplinter. His name is featured on the front cover of this book, and his craft as a writer is on display on every one of its pages. He stepped aboard United to become director of Executive Communications early in my tenure, and from the beginning Brian's prose, verging sometimes into poetry, as well as his sense of humor, gave a great lift to our airline's aspirations, and to my own.

• • •

Of course, my deepest well of gratitude belongs to the people who made this story worth telling in the first place—the members of my own family.

When I said that La Familia is a concept that extends far beyond blood relations, I wasn't kidding. My brothers, sisters, cousins, and everyone else who have shown me so much love and affection throughout my life each deserve their own chapter. But to mention them individually would require telling each of their stories in full, and each would be as extraordinary as the next.

Long before quarantine was a thing, my post-transplant immunocompromised condition kept me isolated from all but the few members of my family and also of Cathy's, who became my caretakers, as well as my source of company and comfort.

"My Heart Leaps Up" is a short poem that contains the famous quote, "The Child is father of the Man." What the poet William Wordsworth meant by this line is that, as adults, we are shaped by our childhoods. I suppose all memoirs are based on this teleology.

While this book often refers to my own childhood, nothing has shaped me more than raising my own children. As I lay dying on that cold apartment floor in Chicago, it was their childhoods that filled my mind. Today, as I live and breathe, nothing makes my heart leap up more than when I think of the adults they've become.

In addition to my oldest, Jessica, I want to pay extra attention to my kids who were a bit younger during the events of this book. Kellie was in her first semester of graduate school at Duke University when she was suddenly called back to Chicago on account of my heart attack. Later, in 2017, the school invited me to give the keynote at its Distinguished Speakers Series, and Kellie introduced me to the assembled students. Sharing a stage with my daughter that day, and to see her speak with such confidence and poise to her fellow graduates, filled me with tears and a sense of pride that only a father can understand.

Kellie and her new husband, Michael Rybak, have just welcomed their firstborn daughter, Scottie Reese, into the world, and I thrill to see them experience the joys of building careers and a family together. Speaking of granddaughters, our first, Emma Lynne, was welcomed into the world by Jessica and her husband, Matt Hall, in 2020. She has been such a source of light and delight in our lives. When she walks into a room and sees me, she'll throw her hands up in the air and yell out, "Poppa," with a smile that could melt the North Pole. These are the joys of being a grandparent, and I hope the stories I tell in this book connect her with where she came from and guide her wherever she goes in life.

My son Kevin has charted his own unique path in life, true to his fearless and independent spirit. After graduating from Vanderbilt in 2017, he deferred many prestigious private-sector job offers, instead choosing to dedicate himself to public service and working on political campaigns. By choosing a path in life that places his political convictions above personal convenience and material gain, he has already made his mark on the world, to the immense pride of his parents. He currently serves as assistant press secretary in the Biden White House, one of the youngest people ever to perform that role.

My youngest son, Jack, who was only beginning high school at the start of this story, is now a senior at my alma mater, USC. He was forced to grow up faster than his siblings, first because I started working in Chicago for United, and even more so when it looked as if I might not survive the heart attack. He chose to spend the school breaks in Chicago so that we could be together, taking part-time summer jobs at our O'Hare operations. Before his first day, I told the team not to show special treatment and assign him the most demanding tasks, just like everyone. His supervisor, Larry Ferrarini, a military veteran with more than five decades of service to

United under his belt, didn't need my permission. He quickly put Jack to work—sorting and loading bags "below the wing," most notably, putting him in the depths of a plane, or belly, during those hot summer months. Before long, he had won Larry's respect, and they remain strong friends to this day.

Jack has a habit for earning people's respect through a combination of cheerfulness and determination, qualities that would make his grandmother Francisca and great-grandmother Josefina proud.

To Cathy, my wife and partner in all things: We struggled together about how, and whether, to write this book, ultimately deciding it was worthwhile. We hoped it might be a gift to others; also, a chronicle of our family's story, something that could be passed on, from one generation to the next. But, secretly, within my own heart, I was determined to write it because it would give me a chance to express my love and gratitude to her, which have grown stronger with each day since I met her as an undergraduate at USC.

Finally, to our employees and customers who continue to kindly approach me during my travels, either in the concourse, in gate areas, or on planes, to offer their appreciation for how United has changed for the better over recent years.

In this book, I tried to capture how much this industry means to so many people. And while harsh criticism comes with the territory, I've found that more often I receive the most generous and welcome votes of thanks, especially from frequent customers.

This book is an attempt to repay that kindness. But the best way to do so—the one I hope is the most lasting legacy of this story—is that people "pave it forward" and offer that "thank you" to the next aviation employee they meet—because that's where the credit belongs.

ABOUT THE AUTHOR

OSCAR MUNOZ served as CEO of United Airlines from September 2015 to May 2020, before becoming executive chairman of the board.

During his tenure as CEO, United achieved a rapid turnaround, delivering industry-leading operational reliability as well as sustained financial success, with its stock value increasing 54 percent during that period. Mr. Munoz himself was credited with reestablishing United's relationship of trust with its own employees as well as the customers and communities they serve. Those efforts earned strong support and praise from United's largest employee unions and resulted in steadily increasing levels of customer satisfaction.

Under Mr. Munoz's leadership, United sustained an impressive track record for leveraging its unique logistical resources and expertise to benefit communities across the United States and around the world, partnering with federal and local entities to deliver vital supplies and personnel where they were needed most—especially during the COVID-19 pandemic. This contribution dramatically expanded the United States' ability to respond to pressing humanitarian crises.

Mr. Munoz also firmly established United, one of the largest carriers by volume, as an aviation industry leader toward achieving an environmentally sustainable future, making historic investments in biofuel technology and next-generation efficient aircraft, as well as seeding innovators on the electric aviation frontier.

As CEO and then as executive chairman, Mr. Munoz helped marshal the global response to the pandemic—partnering with government and administration leaders in support of employees, overseeing the airline's recovery efforts, and working to bring a diverse coalition of people together to create a broad-based, inclusive vision for national economic renewal.

Previously, Oscar served as president and chief operating officer of the North American rail-based transportation supplier CSX Corporation. A decade of excellent financial performance, including a boost in operating income of nearly 600 percent, earned CSX recognition on the list of Most Honored Companies by *Institutional Investor* magazine.

His career spans some of the world's leading consumer brands, from AT&T to Coca-Cola and PepsiCo, as well as US West.

He currently serves on the board of directors of Salesforce, CBRE, TelevisaUnivision, and Archer Aviation, a leading urban air mobility company and developer of all-electric vertical takeoff and landing (eVTOL) aircraft. He is an independent trustee on Fidelity's Equity and High Income Funds board and sits on the Pentagon's Defense Business Board, which is responsible for providing independent advice on business management issues to senior leaders within the Department of Defense.

He is a member of the board of trustees of the Brookings Institution and is also a trustee of the University of Southern California, where he earned his undergraduate degree in business. He also received an MBA from Pepperdine.

Born in Mexico and raised in Southern California, Oscar went on to become the first in his family to attend college. He and his wife, Cathy, founded Pave It Forward, a foundation that raises scholarship funds for students who are also the first in their families to attend a four-year university. The first Latino to run a major US airline, *Hispanic Business* magazine twice named Oscar one of its "100 Most Influential Hispanics."